INTERLINK ILLUSTRATED HISTORIES

Hitler and Nazism

INTERLINK ILLUSTRATED HISTORIES

HITLER

AND NAZISM

ENZO COLLOTTI

Translated by Valerio Lintner

INTERLINK BOOKS

An imprint of Interlink Publishing Group, Inc.
New York

First American edition published in 1999 by

INTERLINK BOOKS
An imprint of Interlink Publishing Group, Inc.
99 Seventh Avenue · Brooklyn, New York 11215 and
46 Crosby Street · Northampton, Massachusetts 01060

Copyright © Giunti Gruppo Editoriale — Casterman, 1995, 1999
Translation copyright © Interlink Publishing/Windrush Press 1999

This edition of *Hitler and Nazism* is published by arrangement
with Giunti Gruppo Editoriale and Casterman Editions.

Library of Congress Cataloging-in-Publication Data
Collotti, Enzo, 1929-
    [Hitler et le Nazisme. English]
    Hitler and Nazism / Enzo Collotti ; translated by Valerio Lintner.
    — 1st American ed.
        p.   cm. — (Interlink illustrated histories)
    Includes bibliographical references and index.
    ISBN 1-56656-238-4
    1. Hitler, Adolf, 1889-1945. 2. National socialism. 3. Germany—
—Politics and government—1918-1933. 4. Germany—Politics and
government—1933-1945. 5. World War, 1933-1945—Germany.
I. Lintner, Valerio. II. Title. III. Series.
DD247.H5C6613   1999
943.086'092–dc21   98-12354
                                                              CIP

Typeset by Archetype IT Ltd., website: www.archetype-it.com
Printed and bound in Italy

To order or request our complete catalog,
please call us at **1-800-238-LINK** or write to:
Interlink Publishing
46 Crosby Street, Northampton, MA 01060
e-mail: interpg@aol.com • website: www.interlinkbooks.com

Contents

HITLER AND NAZISM

Preface

The rise of Nazism was not a chance event, as it was sometimes taken to be in historical literature outside Germany, especially during the Second World War. At that time there was a tendency to emphasize a continuity between Lutheran reform and Nazism, almost to the point of insisting on the systematic separation of German history from that of Western Europe. This view bears a striking resemblance to that found in nationalist and conservative historical writing, which was, not surprisingly, embraced by the Nazis. For them, the "particular path" (*Sonderweg*) involved not only consolidating Germany as a great power, but also the rejection of models of institutional and social organization (for example the parliamentary system) considered to be alien to the traditions and character of the German people.

The triumph of Nazism should instead be seen in the light of the failure of the first attempt to democratize German society in the wake of the First World War and the crisis in the German Empire. An important factor in this failed attempt was the peace settlement reached at Versailles. This represented one of the most serious obstacles to the establishment of Weimar democracy, imposing on Germany not only territorial losses but also considerable social and economic burdens (reparation payments), as well as military restrictions (the abolition of conscription, reductions in the armed forces, and the demilitarization of the Rhineland).

The identification of the democratic republic with military defeat and a punitive peace weakened the credibility of democratic development in the eyes of the mass of the population. This opened up the possibility for the forces of nationalism and traditional anti-Semitism to group together, under the flag of offended national pride, all the humiliations and frustrations of those who had suffered in the war, and who were now disturbed and confused by the post-war political and economic crisis, and by the crisis in values implicit in institutional reform.

The history of National Socialism is thus first and foremost a part of the history of twentieth-century Germany. In the short term it emerged from the crisis in the Weimar Republic and the failure of the democratic experiment attempted after the Great War. In the long term it involved the tensions between state and society which had lain behind the problems of the political system ever since the unification of the various German states into one empire and the creation of the Second Reich. It also encompassed the problem of determining the international position of Germany, which before the First World War had oscillated between the desire to built a *Weltpolitik* and the more modest option of filling a hegemonic role in east-central and south-eastern Europe, exploiting its geopolitical position and economic power rather than adopting any ideologically-motivated plan for domination.

But the history of National Socialism also largely transcends national boundaries, on at least two counts. Because Nazism took to its logical conclusion the desire to create a strong state as an essential prerequisite for the expansion of German influence, its attempt at domination disrupted the whole of the continent of Europe, and, with the outbreak of the Second World War, the entire world order.

Secondly, the history of Nazism is an integral and certainly not insignificant part of the process which led to the emergence of totalitarian states of a Fascist nature in Europe between the wars. Nazism significantly influenced the nature of these regimes, although one should not underestimate the particular features of other similar regimes as well as the specific characteristics of German Nazism.

The creation of the totalitarian state in Germany is of great importance, as is the gradual way in which steps towards dictatorship were implemented: the institutional changes of 1933–35, consolidation between 1934 and 1938, and finally the adoption of the instruments of dictatorship as the ideological and material basis for racism and Nazi imperialism between 1939 and 1945. Because of this, it is principally on the nature of the system and the development of its internal dynamics that we will concentrate our attention in this book.

Enzo Collotti

Chapter 1

CRISIS IN THE
WEIMAR REPUBLIC AND
THE RISE OF NAZISM

AT THE END OF THE 1920S, THE FAILURE OF THE WEIMAR DEMOCRATIC REPUBLIC PRECIPITATED AN UNPRECEDENTED ECONOMIC, SOCIAL AND POLITICAL CRISIS IN GERMANY. THIS PERMITTED THE RAPID RISE TO POWER OF THE EXTREME NATIONALIST AND RACIST RIGHT.

The ascent to power of National Socialism was certainly due to the strength of the National Socialist Party of German Workers (NSDAP) and the socio-political forces whose rebellious tendencies and deep anti-democratic potential the party succeeded in unifying and harnessing. It was also a result of the process of disintegration into which the democratic republic had fallen, shaken by the political crises which had continually dogged its path, and even more by the decay in its social fabric caused by the economic paralysis that struck Germany at the end of the 1920s. This was a product of the Great Depression which hit both the American economy and the many countries which after the First World War had developed ever closer relationships and ties with the USA.

Social, Political and Institutional Crisis

The crisis in the Weimar Republic was not just a political one involving policies and attitudes. It was rather the result of a collapse of the balance between the social and political forces on which the political system of the 1919 constitution had been based for a decade. At the time the Weimar constitution was, along with the

The Versailles Treaty, signed on 28 June 1919 at the end of the First World War, imposed heavy conditions on Germany, which was considered "responsible for all the loss and devastations suffered by the Allied governments". These conditions included the cession of Alsace-Lorraine and the Saar mines, a drastic reduction of the army, the elimination of the fleet, and payment of 269 million golden marks as reparation for war damages. The National Socialist Party focused the discontent of a large section of the population on the rejection of the Versailles Treaty. The picture shows a mass demonstration against the Versailles Treaty in Berlin in 1919; the banner, hinting at President Wilson's engagements, reads "Only the 14 points".

Ph. © Publiphoto

Berlin: electoral propaganda by the Social Democratic Party for the elections of 19 January 1919. Candidates were elected by universal suffrage and women had obtained the right to vote; the constitution, proclaimed in August, instituted a parliamentary democracy. Below: the Weimar National Assembly.
Ph. © Publifoto

Austrian constitution, the most advanced example of a democratic constitution to have emerged in Europe in the post-war period. In establishing a republic based on parliamentary democracy and a mutually interdependent relationship between the economy and the infrastructure of employment, it embarked on a process of transforming the old institutional structure and traditional power relationships. In practice this transformation was only partially realized.

The political crisis in the democratic republic was manifested in a permanent tension between the impetus towards change and reform on the one hand, and the moves towards conservatism and preservation of the *status quo* on the other. This effectively precluded the ambitious plans for democratization of state and society contained in the constitution, in both letter and spirit.

The most obvious and important impediment to full implementation of the principles of the constitution lay in the continuing presence of conservatism in key areas of government such as schools, universities and the judiciary, as well as in the armed forces, where reform had been no more than superficial. The bureaucracy was in many ways still wedded to the spirit and authoritarian traditions of the monarchy, and had neither the background nor the necessary

will to act as an effective support for the new democratic institutions. In addition, the very functions of the bureaucracy were altered in the context of a new relationship between the newly-representative political powers and the executive.

The principle was that the bureaucracy should no longer be the arbiter of conflicts and regulatory powers which affected the population, but rather the guarantor of both the functioning of the administration and the rights of citizens. This principle frequently aroused the hostility of older civil servants, who were not in sympathy with the spirit of democracy. Teachers ridiculed the egalitarian tendencies of the democratic republic, which in 1919 had abolished the privileges of the aristocracy and other select groups, and had given women the vote. Judges continued to reject the right to basic freedoms (freedom of the press, freedom of assembly, freedom of expression) that had been established by the constitution, behaving as if no institutional change had taken place in 1919. They continued to use old principles of class and social status to deny social rights and new interpretations of the right to property which were demanded by the constitution.

The most obvious area in which the conflict between the new system and former authoritarian tendencies surfaced was over the reorganization of the armed forces. The republic formally abolished the autonomy of the military to act as a state within a state or as the armed wing of an authoritarian monarchy. Civil power replaced military power. In reality there was a somewhat ambiguous re-evaluation of the military and its

Karl Liebknecht was, with Rosa Luxemburg, among the founders of the Spartakusbund, *core of the future German Communist Party. Imprisoned for pacifism in 1916 and freed in 1918, he took part in the "Spartacist Revolution" in Berlin between 5 and 12 January 1919. Captured by the volunteer corps with Rosa Luxemburg, he was shot on 15 January 1919. The picture shows Liebknecht speaking to the crowd at the Berlin Teptower Park in 1918.*

social role. The old imperial army ranks were maintained, and the republic's politicians themselves showed certain reservations about the after-effects of the Versailles treaty. But, faced with Spartacist and Soviet uprisings during the winter of 1918–19, the republican authorities had to call on units of the old army as well as new armed groups (including the volunteer corps) recruited from Great War veterans and young adherants of a new anti-Bolshevik and anti-Semitic tendency, in trying to establish order.

The appointment of old Field Marshal Hindenburg as President in April 1925 represented a reversal of republican values. A nostalgic monarchist, the new President was a figurehead for the vengeful spirit of the old establishment, such as the old military ranks, the Prussian aristocracy and the large land-

Above: Rosa Luxemburg (1870–1919).
Below: a satirical cartoon by George Grosz, ironically titled The Triumph of Republican Thought.

"Der Sieg des republikanischen Gedankens"

Von Noske begrüsst

Von Loebe empfangen

Von Ebert gerufen

owners of the eastern provinces. Hindenburg's election highlighted the conflict within the constitution between the democratic principle and its radical plebiscite element. The intention to legitimize the chief executive by means of popular consensus did not prove to be a democratizing factor: the electorate used democracy to express a typically anti-democratic option.

Electing Hindenburg also meant electing the values he represented and to which he always remained faithful. Later, when the crisis exploded fully in 1930, he was to use the exceptional powers provided by Article 48 of the Weimar constitution to legitimize the extra-parliamentarian administration of Chancellor Brüning. He not only made use of the instruments provided by the constitution, but also took advantage of those instruments to marginalize parliament.

Field Marshal Paul von Beneckendorff und von Hindenburg, head of the armed forces during the First World War. He was elected President in 1925 and re-elected in 1932 at the age of eighty-five. Below: a coin worth fifty million marks, issued in 1923 in the middle of the economic crisis.
Ph. © Publiphoto

Economic Crisis and Mass Unemployment

Between 1925 and 1929 economic stabilization resulted in a collapse of the social peace agreed at the end of 1918 between trade unions and industrialists, in the wake of institutional reform. By the same token, the outbreak of an economic crisis in 1930 marked the abandonment by the relevant economic forces of all reservation and moderation. In the field of social unity, the failure by the republic to implement reforms — such as the expropriation of large land estates and the socialization of important industries — which had been promised before the collapse of the empire, strengthened the social role and contractual power of agricultural and industrial employers alike.

In 1920 inflation was at catastrophic levels: the dollar reached a record value of 4.2 billion marks. The mayor of Berlin wrote in his diary: "Hoards of the unemployed in front of the town hall, riots for food in the city." Above: a workers' demonstration in Berlin.
Ph. © Publiphoto
Below: a procession of the unemployed.

At the peak of the crisis, both these groups opposed the democratic republic. The *ostelbisch* landowners (those to the east of the Elbe), undergoing a crisis which involved their very existance and which therefore went beyond pure economics, did not limit themselves to milking the state treasury, but also rejected the land reform which had been proposed even by conservative politicians. In the same way, in the middle of the crisis industrial employers re-established their freedom of manoeuvre and emphasized the weakness of the state, which was one of the most important characteristics of the Weimar system. Thus the new rapport between the state and the economy which was established after the Great War totally precluded the state from acting as an arbitrator and a mediator of social conflicts.

Following alarming job cuts in manufacturing industries now deprived of American capital, tensions in the labour market reached unprecedented levels. In 1932 nearly one in two German workers was unemployed. This was a terrible blow for German society, even worse than the inflation which it had suffered after the war. Mass unemployment at the levels reached in the years between 1930 and 1932 was something new. It destabilized families and professions, parties and trade unions, both psychologically and materially. It affected economic and cultural life. It reshaped the mentalities and behaviour of classes and individuals. It particularly affected collective behaviour, discredited democracy and, with the sense of general insecurity it encouraged demagogy and political speculation.

The Rise of the National Socialist Party

The great beneficiary of the crisis was the National Socialist Party. The party had originated in the immediate post-war period from a rudimentary German workers' party created in Munich at the beginning of 1919 by the Bavarian nationalist and anti-Semitic movement. The National Socialist Party of German Workers (the *National-Sozialistische Deutsche Arbeiter Partei*, NSDAP), as it was renamed on 24 February 1920, at first represented a modest nucleus of war veterans, the unemployed, and the lower working classes. Here Adolf Hitler, then a lance-corporal in the Reichswehr, cut his political teeth. Driving out its original leaders, Hitler became the head of the party in July 1921. He thus tied his destiny to that of the NSDAP and the latter's destiny to that of

The volunteer corps were armed troops who mostly came from the army and were protected by it. They took on the task of defending Germany's eastern frontiers against the Bolsheviks. When creating storm troops or Sturmabteilungen known as the SA, Ernst Röhm recruited most of its members from the volunteer corps. The picture shows a procession of volunteer corps with Adolf Hitler (inset).
Ph. © Publiphoto

Adolf Hitler was born in Braunau in High Austria on 20 April 1889; he came from a modest lower-middle-class family (his father was a Customs officer). He finished his education in Linz and then moved to Vienna in 1907, the year of his mother's death (his father had died in 1903); he lived there between 1908 and 1912, doing occasional drawings and watercolours, after failing to get into the Figurative Arts Academy. In Vienna, already troubled by the problems of multi-culturalism, he acquired the anti-socialist and anti-Semitic hatred which, as he himself stated in the autobiographical part of *Mein Kampf,* deeply affected the formation of his political ideas. In 1912 he moved to Munich, where he was caught up in the First World War — an event that was to precipitate his political involvement. He fought as a volunteer in the Bavarian army and was wounded on a number of occasions. The violence, sacrifice and excitement of war, together with the military discipline it necessitated, seemed ideally suited to his desire for order and to the savage vitality with which he

embraced racist propaganda. In March 1919 in Munich, on the eve of the proclamation of the Weimar Republic, he actively participated in counter-revolutionary repression, and in the following September he established contacts with Anton Drexler's *Deutsche Arbeiter-Partei.* Acting as a political agitator, from the spring of 1920 he concerned himself primarily with party propaganda, and in February renamed the party the National Socialist Party of German Workers (NSDAP). In spring 1921 he became the undisputed head of the party, thanks to his violent nationalist speeches against Versailles and the Weimar

Republic, which attracted the support of disappointed members of the traditional right. Following the failure of the 8–9 November 1923 putsch, which should have resulted in a march on Berlin, he only served part of the five-year prison sentence he was given on 1 April 1924. When, at the end of the same year, he left the Landsberg fortress, he had completed the first part of the work in which he outlined his political beliefs — *Mein Kampf.* It was published between 1925 and 1926. By February 1925 he was again the undisputed head of the NSDAP, a position he strengthened in the following years as he eliminated personal rivals and tendencies opposed to his leadership, including, in 1930, the "left" of Otto and Gregor Strasser. His rise, which was linked to the crisis of the Weimar Republic debilitated by the Great Depression, was facilitated by his acquisition of German citizenship thanks to his appointment as a government official in Brunswick in February 1932.

After January 1933, when he was awarded the Reich Chancellorship by Field Marshal Hindenburg, his fate became inextricably linked with the history of Nazi Germany. While

Adolf Hitler shaking hands with the exultant crowd after a speech. Below: Hitler and Eva Braun with their dogs in 1945. Opposite: a portrait of Hitler in 1921.
Ph. © Publiphoto

consolidating the dictatorship, Hitler strengthened his own personal power with the elimination of his most dangerous rival — the SA leader Röhm. When Hindenburg died, on 2 August 1934, Hitler became head of state. In February 1938 he took direct command of the Wehrmacht on the eve of the world war he himself provoked. The war, by further unifying the nation around the Führer and the regime, increased the concentration of power in his hands, especially after the defeats on the Eastern Front which fuelled his distrust of senior army officers. It was in fact the military, supported by some in administrative and diplomatic circles, who plotted the attempt on his life on 20 July 1944. This he survived, responding with a bloody repression and ordering resistance to the bitter end. He started a "scorched earth" policy in front of the enemy now invading Germany from both east and west. His final speech, in which he handed his powers over to Admiral Dönitz, was a reiteration of his anti-Bolshevism and anti-Semitism; he then committed suicide in the bunker of the Chancellery in Berlin on 30 April 1945. Eva Braun, whom he had married the day before, died with him. Medical documentation provided by the Soviet Union at the end of 1968 seems to have definitively wiped out any lingering doubts over Hitler's death. ■

Germany, establishing as a main objective the extension of the party's sphere of influence to the Bavarian region and then to the entire Reich.

Before discussing the broad outlines of the NSDAP's political rise, it is important to analyze the programme it presented on 24 February 1920. It was on the basis of this programme, with some occasional changes over the years, that the party built its political fortune, to the point of attracting wide-ranging support and taking power on the basis of this popular support. What immediately strikes one in the programme of 24 February, even in the context of the traditional ultra-nationalist right, was the force and coherence with which the principles of a new, specifically anti-Semitic racism were proclaimed. The programme made explicit references to the peace treaties, and in particular rejected the Treaty of Versailles. In this way the NSDAP hoped to harness and exploit the nationalist leanings of a large segment of the German population — especially the middle classes, who dreamed of a Greater

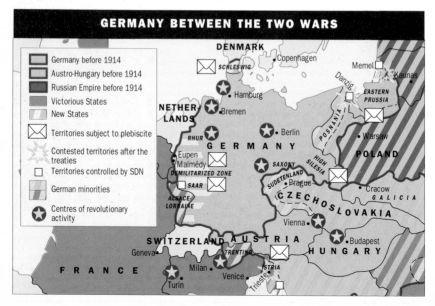

GERMANY BETWEEN THE TWO WARS

Germany before 1914
Austro-Hungary before 1914
Russian Empire before 1914
Victorious States
New States
Territories subject to plebiscite
Contested territories after the treaties
Territories controlled by SDN
German minorities
Centres of revolutionary activity

Germany which, by regaining its colonies and extending its territory, would become a world power.

This imperialistic expansion was linked to a definition of the German people as a race, and anticipated the division and discrimination among citizens brought about by the Nazi regime. Jews were declared alien to the German-blooded population. As such they were to be deprived of citizenship and excluded, not only from political (and even civil) rights, but especially from public appointments, including the Press. Anti-Semitism had traditionally been given considerable social and cultural importance in German society since the first half of the nineteenth century; but now, for the first time in history, it was to become one of the cornerstones of political life, a codified form of state racism. This development was linked, in Germany as elsewhere, to the publication in 1919 and

subsequent dissemination of an outrageous fabrication of international anti-Semitism, *The Protocols of the Sages of Zion*.

In spite of some anti-capitalist and demagogic elements, the National Socialist Party programme soon proved popular with the commercial and rural middle and lower-middle classes. It also suited the interests of white-collar workers in the big cities, who saw Nazism as a bulwark against Bolshevism. The photo shows Communists being arrested in Berlin in 1933.

Vaguely anti-capitalist in its first draft and inspired by populist elements, the first NSDAP platform used such slogans as "common good before individual good" and "eliminate the dependency on profit". However, in 1928 Hitler modified his previously-proclaimed principle of land reform without compensation. The principle was now applied uniquely to the detriment of Jewish speculators.

In reality, Hitler's effort to gain consensus and attract people who wanted to exploit his appeal and use violence against the Weimar democracy served to establish a direct method

of action against labour organizations and left-wing democratic groups. The first phase of the NS-DAP's rise to power coincided with the years in which the consequences of the Versailles treaty were most evident. These years saw a violent nationalistic reaction to Allied policy (especially after the occupation of the Ruhr in January 1923), paving the way for the most disturbing elements among war veterans to group around the small National Socialist Party. They were attracted by the paramilitary structure with which the party intended to fight against the Weimar Republic. Hitler's collaborators already included Hermann Goering, an ex-captain in the First World War airforce who would become the most important man in the Third Reich after Hitler himself. Among other party members the name of General Ludendorff stood out. He was a racist and later a theorist of "total war". He was never integrated fully into official Nazism, but he was a symbol of what the NSDAP wanted to achieve and, above all, the scourge of everything to which it was fanatically opposed.

Above: A French tank in Frankfurt during the Ruhr occupation. Below: General Ludendorff is applauded by the crowd as he leaves the courthouse after his acquittal on charges relating to the Munich putsch on 8–9 November 1923. Ph. © Publiphoto

Bavarian pride and hostility to the Reich, in the shape of the democratic republic, exploded dramatically in the attempted Munich *putsch* of 8–9 November 1923, which saw Hitler and Ludendorff working side by side against the Bavarian police and Reichswehr forces. The Beer Hall *putsch* was rapidly suppressed and the NSDAP,

which already had 50,000 members, was outlawed.

In March 1924 the trial of Hitler and others involved in the *putsch* resulted in a politically unsatisfactory outcome. Ludendorff was acquitted, saved by his own fame; Hitler was sentenced to five years in prison, but by the end of 1924 he was already free. In prison he wrote what became the bible of National Socialism, *Mein Kampf,* published between 1925 and 1926. The party survived underground. At the Reichstag elections of 7 December 1924 it was presented as the National Socialist movement for freedom, gaining 900,000 votes — three per cent of the electorate. After capturing 2.6 per cent of the vote in the 1928 elections, the NSDAP made a big jump in the 1930 elections with 18.3 per cent of the vote. It was now an important nationalist and anti-democratic force opposed to the Weimar system.

The party sought the support of the upper classes, who saw in the NSDAP an organization with the ability to translate the rhetoric of the democratic and progressive forces of the traditional right into concrete initiatives, following the example of the Fascist *squadrismo* developed in Italy and other European countries. However, the National Socialist Party was increasingly also becoming attractive to the middle classes who were hostile to the demo-

> *"It would be human and natural for the state to place race at the centre of general existence. The state must assure the purity of the race."*
>
> Mein Kampf

Left: Hitler during his imprisonment in the Landsberg fortress. Above: a copy of Mein Kampf, *on which some of the most important Nazi officials swore an oath of loyalty to the Führer.*

On 3 August 1921 Hitler created his storm troops, the SA. Recruited predominantly from the ranks of former First World War soldiers, the SA constituted the military wing of the NSDAP and used squad attack methods to implement Nazi anti-Semitism and anti-Bolshevism. Below: E. Heines, party secretary in Silesia, who was killed during the purge of 30 June 1934.
Ph. © Publiphoto

cratic republic. Research into the electorate during the years of the crisis of the Weimar Republic, and into the social composition of the NSDAP, confirms this analysis.

The Collapse of Traditional Political Parties

In parallel with the worsening economic crisis (significant indicators falling below acceptable levels: national income below the lowest post-war level; industrial production almost half that of more stable years; wages half those of 1929, which was considered the last year of relative normality), came the disintegration of the social fabric and fragmentation of the political and party system. The crisis saw the rise of increasingly violent forms of social protest. The organizations of employed workers were opposed by angry and desperate masses of the unemployed, which left trade unions unable to reconcile contrasting interests.

Politics, too, acquired unusually radical features. In the face of a system unable to correct its dysfunctions and give convincing answers to the problems thrown up by the crisis, forces which aimed purely and simply to destroy the democratic republic emerged. On the one hand there were the paramilitary groups of the National Socialist Party (the SA — *Sturmabteilungen* or storm troops), which identified with a populist tendency, represented anti-capitalism, and used direct action and terrorist attacks in the streets against political enemies in the widest sense — including organized labour, the democratic intelligentsia, and pacifists.

On the other hand, forces were created which would constitute the political bloc supporting the rise to power of the NSDAP. The platform of the so-called "national opposition", which found expression in the Harzburg Front of 11 October 1931, paved the way for an alliance of the historical right and the new right as an alternative to the Weimar system. The Harzburg Front bloc was the political expression of several social groups whose interests, diverse as they were, converged to reject democracy. The traditional right of the German National Party presided over by Alfred Hugenberg — an industrialist and mass communications tycoon, who used his power to influence and manipulate public opinion against the

democratic republic — was hand in hand with the new right of the National Socialist Party. Alongside them stood the powerful fighting organization of the "helmets of steel" (*Stahlhelm*); plus some prestigious figures from the military and financial world, in particular General von Seeckt and the ex-President of the Reichsbank, Hjalmar Schacht.

The axis established between Hugenberg and

*A*bove: *members of the Harzburg Front in October 1931. Below: members of the Stahlhelm taking the oath. The "steel helmets" were a paramilitary organization of ex-soldiers — President Hindenburg was their honorary commander.*
Ph. © Publiphoto

A secret meeting with Ruhr industrialists before the 1932 elections was persistently denied by Hitler. The picture shows the Ruhr magnates at Düsseldorf in the Rhineland, site of the meeting.
Ph. © Publiphoto.

Hitler, between the *Stahlhelm* and Schacht, meant that the National Socialist Party was no longer isolated. An important element in the opposition to the republic, it was no longer considered as a dangerous rival to the traditional right, but almost as an avant-garde attacking force behind which the traditional right now wanted to operate. The party played the role of battering-ram which the traditionalists were incapable of undertaking themselves. The consensus built by the NSDAP in the provinces among middle-and lower-middle-class craftsmen and shopkeepers was now supplemented by the landowners of the eastern provinces,

and by a substantial proportion of white-collar workers and business people in the big cities who were erstwhile supporters of the German National Party. The NSDAP allowed these groups to unite their often contrasting interests, especially around key issues of nationalistic appeal, such as the violent campaign against the Versailles treaty.

Above all, it was the NSDAP's new brand of anti-Semitism that attracted the masses who had never been won over by the republic and were especially hit and disorientated by the crisis. The NSDAP blamed the crisis on the Jews; by ousting Jews from their jobs and positions the party would ensure work for the rest of the population. This was clearly ridiculous in a situation in which forty per cent of people of working age were unemployed and Jews represented barely one per cent of the German population, but gives an idea of the new values developed by Hitler's party with the collaboration of the other forces of the "national opposition".

The Nazi Party, which was now aiming to conquer the state, enjoyed the support of the old traditional right. This proved to be the most significant element in the Reichstag elections of 31 July 1932. At the peak of its electoral fortunes the NSDAP had 37.4 per cent of the vote, mainly as a result of the collapse of the German National Party, the German Popular Party and the liberals of the Democratic Party. The NSDAP was growing from the ruins of traditional middle class parties, with the exception of the Catholic Centre Party. In the elections of 6 November 1932 the NSDAP fell back (to 33.1 per cent), but kept a relative majority, in contrast to all the other parties, which suffered a resounding defeat. Thus, although it was true that the NSDAP did not obtain the expected consensus, nothing could now oppose its rise to government. In a petition on 19 November 1932, industrialists and landowners invited President Hindenburg — who could not ignore their demands — to put Hitler at the head of the new government. This would consolidate the "national movement" which, by eliminating social conflicts, would allow German economic recovery.

Above: electoral propaganda poster for the Reichstag elections on 31 July 1932. Hitler promises well-being and happiness to all Germans: "We take the nation's destiny in our hands". Below: a poster for the presidential elections in April 1932 invites votes for Hindenburg: "Down with Hitler's popular agitation".
Ph. © Publiphoto

Chapter 2
THE ESTABLISHMENT
OF THE DICTATORSHIP

BY EXPLOITING THE ALLIANCE WITH THE FORCES OF THE TRADITIONAL RIGHT, AND HAVING SILENCED THE OPPOSITION OF THE WEIMAR PARTIES AND THE INTERNAL REBELLION OF ITS MOST EXTREME FRINGES, THE NSDAP PROCEEDED TO DISMANTLE FEDERAL STRUCTURES, CONCENTRATING POWER INCREASINGLY IN THE HANDS OF THE FÜHRER.

T he Nazi dictatorship was not built in a day. It was constructed gradually, partly following a plan and partly as a reaction to circumstances. Was this a seizure of power on the Nazis' part or a simple transition of power to Nazism?

This debate, which is more than merely a semantic one has stimulated German historiography over the last decade and has helped to clarify the material process by which the Nazis became established in power, as well as specifying the nature of the crisis in the Weimar system. However, it does not alter the fact that the turning point came on 30 January 1933, when President Hindenburg assigned the Chancellery to the Nazi Führer.

From the Burning of the Reichstag to Total Power

For both internal and external reasons, Hitler's prime preoccupation was to give an impression of moderation when starting the process of change which he had been appointed to implement. The first government he formed consisted largely of a coalition cabinet of the old forces of "national opposition". Representatives of the Nazi Party

Nobody took more care than Hitler in the choice of his party's emblems: it seems that to find a model of an eagle to use as an official rubber stamp he turned the heraldry section of the Munich library upside down. Opposite: a gigantic eagle is erected in an exhibition hall. Ph. © Publiphoto

Above: Hitler receives a handshake from President Hindenburg after his nomination as Chancellor.
Right: Hitler in conversation with two members of his first government — General von Blomberg, Minister for War (on the right), and vice-Chancellor Franz von Papen.
Ph. © Publiphoto

were in the minority. By opening up the government to the nation's conservatives, Hitler created a sort of political broad right alliance. Von Papen was appointed as vice-Chancellor, Hugenberg as Minister for the Economy and von Neurath as Foreign Minister; all appeared to be the new government's guarantors of good faith towards the conservative group which had supported the Nazi anti-Weimar campaign. The army wasn't forgotten either: General von Blomberg was appointed as Minister for the Reichswehr, and the veterans were represented in the government by Franz Seldte, the head of the *Stahlhelm*, who was made Minister for Employment.

The government platform was thus arranged along the lines of an alliance between Nazism and traditional élites: an alliance which was to represent a stabilizing factor in the regime. What united these élites with Nazism, both negatively (an aversion towards common enemies) and positively (the objective of replacing the democratic republic with a conservative regime, and dreams of the renaissance of Greater Germany as a military power), was stronger than that which divided them. In this sense Field Marshal Hindenburg, in his role as

President, played the part of a guarantor, an effect that would continue even after the death of the old President. However, the policy of implementing political transition by both acquiring the support of influential conservatives and gaining a popular mandate in the polling booths was only partly successful.

The election called for 5 March 1933 took place in the middle of a terrorist campaign. On the night of 27 February the burning of the Reichstag, the true instigators of which are still not known – although it is clear that the Nazis benefited – provided the pretext for the President of the Reich to issue a first decree. This deeply affected civic and political rights and restored the death penalty for a series of crimes against the state. The timing of the announcement of this first decree on 28 February supports the hypothesis that it had been prepared in advance, to be passed at the first opportunity. It even gives credence to the suspicion that the fire itself was premeditated.

The decree of 28 February was the first of many provisions by which the Weimar constitutional system was dismantled without ever being formally repealed. The abolition of civil rights, the concen-

"The Reichstag is burning! The Communists have set it on fire! This will be the fate of the whole country if Communists and Social Democrats get into power in a few months!" So proclaimed the leaflet (below) posted on Hitler's orders on the morning following the burning of the Reichstag. Above: the Reichstag in ruins.

Ph. © Publiphoto

Der Reichstag in Flammen!

Von Kommunisten in Brand gesteckt!

So würde das ganze Land aussehen, wenn der Kommunismus und die mit ihm verbündete Sozialdemokratie auch nur auf ein paar Monate an die Macht kämen!

Braue Bürger als Geiseln an die Wand gestellt! Den Bauern den roten Hahn aufs Dach gesetzt!

Wie ein Aufschrei muß es durch Deutschland gehen:

Zerstampft den Kommunismus! Zerschmettert die Sozialdemokratie!

Wählt **Hitler 1** Liste

tration of power to control every part of the state and society, and the marginalization of legislative power in the face of an ever more powerful executive, can be considered the three key factors in the transformation of the political and constitutional system.

In spite of the show of strength by Nazism in power, the results of the elections which they entirely controlled from above were less favourable than they had expected: they did obtain 43.9 per cent of the vote, but not the unanimous mandate to which they aspired. It is true,

Veterans of the 1870 war, escorted by militants of the Stahlhelm, approach the Potsdam garrison church on 21 March 1933.

however, that their votes were supplemented by the secondary, but not insignificant, vote for the national conservatives who collaborated in Hitler's cabinet. The consequences of the situation created by the election of the new Reichstag were serious. At their inaugural meeting, parliament suffered its first abuse and its first curtailment of power: the eighty-one Communist representatives who had been elected, despite every terrorist pressure, were immediately turned away, without even being allowed to step into the hall. Parliament was becoming a mere fiction. In the following months the representatives of the Social Democratic Party and Centre Party declined in number, as the culmination to the process of dissolution and self-dissolution that had been imposed on the old Weimar political parties.

The opening of the new Reichstag on 21 March, the so-called "Day of Potsdam", allowed the regime to cloak itself in the legitimacy of the Prussian military tradition. It was a foretaste of how the regime was to manipulate the people, and the basis of many of its public manifestations, but it was also the beginning of the decline in the Reichstag's powers. On 24 March 1933, with only the Social Democratic representatives still present to oppose the motion, the Reichstag voted for its own political suicide by handing over full powers to Hitler. In effect this meant that the Reichstag was relinquishing its own right to be the holder of legislative power. This was delegated to the government of the Reich and through it to the person of the Führer and Chancellor. In this way, without the need to repeal the Weimar constitution, the Nazi government claimed unlimited power to modify constitutional norms. It transferred to itself from then on an almost absolute power to legislate and to modify the political system, as well as to abolish constitutional guarantees.

Despite this action, one could not yet see the real lines of the new system which was destined to replace the old one, but all lines were laid down for the destruction and dismantlement of the old structures. In particular, the absence of any checks allowed the new executive a free hand in every field of legislation and administration, thus anticipating the final realization of a power monopoly in the hands of the National Socialist Party. The NSDAP had constantly placed the dual objectives of the capture of the state and the domination of society at the heart of its political objectives.

One of the first of the spectacular parades which, under the expert direction of Goebbels, were to become an essential part of the regime's choreography was the SA march through the Brandenburg Gate on the night of 30 January 1933.
Ph. © Publiphoto

The Creation of a Totalitarian State

With the dismantlement of the old system, the bulk of the new institutions were reorganized along a few basic principles: the monopoly of power of the Nazi Party; the concentration of all powers at the top; and the recognition of the Führer's function as the leader and symbol of a strongly hierarchical system (*Führerprinzip*).

Adolf Hitler portrayed by the Mexican painter Diego Rivera (1886–1957), in a 1933 painting.

In March 1933 the concentration camps came into operation; the prisons were no longer sufficient to hold the thousands of individuals, party officials, intellectuals and militants whom the regime wanted to "re-educate".

An essential part of this process was the abolition of the old parties, whether by self-destruction (as in the case of the Centre Party), or by force (as happened with the Social Democratic Party). The logic of this development was clear: it was a matter of depriving any factor which could represent a potential source of opposition of its legitimacy. The disbandment of these parties also purged the Reichstag of any traditional political representation. The sovereignty of the people was, of necessity, a principle alien to the nature of the Nazi system, which was typically anti-egalitarian and elitist, based not on consensus but on hierarchy, not on the will of the people but on the supremacy of the race.

The fate of political enemies (and not only racial ones) was not only to be marginalized, but also to be humiliated and physically annihilated. This was part of the new method of political warfare launched by the NSDAP and now close to becoming state practice. In March 1933 concentration camps began to function. Prisons were no longer big enough to lock up the tens of thousands of individuals, party officials, intellectuals and militants whom the government at first allegedly wanted to "re-educate".

As the old party system was eliminated, political and institutional space was opened up for the National Socialist Party. A law of 14 July 1933 forbade the creation of political parties and proclaimed the NSDAP to be the sole authorized party. This was merely a foretaste of the principle of the unity of the state and the party which was to be proclaimed on the following 1 December. A law of 7 April had already defined the criteria for the purging of public administration, allowing the expulsion from the system of all who had been loyal to the Weimar Republic as well as officials of "non-Aryan origin"; reinforced by the new law on the role of the Nazi Party, this helped to introduce the monopoly control of every political function to which the Nazis aspired. In this way the process of controlling the state was legitimized. Members of the National Socialist Party seized key posts in all administrative sectors, with hardly any dissent or serious problems — due partly to the conformity and timidity of many officials.

But it was not only the control of the administration which assured political and social rule. Alongside the monopoly of political and administrative power went a monopoly on information, which was fundamental to ensure the control of public opinion. Control of the flow of information was centralized, as was the direction of communication media. The NSDAP's monopoly finally meant the end of any pluralism even in the field of leisure activities, which had been one of

"Germany listens to the Führer through the people's broadcast": this leaflet invites people to listen to the radio in order to develop a Nazi spirit. Goebbels methodically exploited the radio as a means of mass persuasion.

Opposite: above, vice-Chancellor von Papen; below, a member of the Hitlerjugend during specialist training in radio communications.
Ph. © Publiphoto

the privileged areas of the growing labour movement during the Weimar years. The decrease in working hours had given a decisive momentum to the development of cultural output, in an age of mass society and increased leisure time, and also of organized workers' access to cultural, sporting and tourist activities. The NSDAP's monopoly left no freedom of choice in this field: the Nazi Party and the closely-related Labour Front extended their control over all leisure activity for workers, young people and women alike, with the objective of shaping them in its own image.

Typical of a mass party with a rigidly hierarchic and authoritarian structure, without any element of internal democracy, the NSDAP owed its cohesion not only to ideological factors, but also to the bellicose and militarized glamour with which it was

associated. It is clear that after its rise to power the NSDAP underwent an almost physiological process of growth, thanks to the many who found solace or protection in the collective identity of the militants. This had the effect of creating a large and passive consensus of opinion. The important thing for the regime, however, was to stop the pressure or poten-

Above: girls form a huge swastika during a gymnastic demonstration in Nuremberg in 1934.
Ph. © Publiphoto

tial for opposition. For this it needed a strong core of militants, but it also needed to count on that passive consensus to help guarantee political and social control over the populace.

The destruction of local authorities had been an essential part of this process, more than a mere passing phase. The destruction of the *Länder*, the federal structure created by the 1919 constitution, was one of the priorities for a regime which had the totalitarian ambitions of the Nazis. This was not only due to the abstract principle of the concentration of power but to the centralization of methods and the creation of an ideal state inspired by principles of conformity as well as hierarchy.

The Weimar experience had shown that the autonomy of the *Länder* could favour the development of opposition and of diverse political circumstances which would provide an alternative to central government. The most glamorous case had been the Prussian *Land* which, having been territorially and legally cut down to the size of the other *Länder* in the 1919 constitution, had taken on a very different role than that assigned to it by history. Strangely enough, during the Weimar years Prussia had been one of the bulwarks of democracy in Germany, the *Land* where the democratic spectre of Weimar stubbornly persisted in regional government. It was no accident that the

coup on 20 July 1932 through which the then Chancellor von Papen intervened *manu militari* to dissolve the Prussian government happened in the most troubled phase of the Weimar crisis. It was regarded as a real assault against republican legality and the ability of democratic institutions to prevent their own dissolution.

The NSDAP understood very well, after the failure of the precipitate and amateurish 1923 Munich coup, that a strategy of slow deception was required to move them closer to power. Political convergence with Hugenberg's German nationalists and the slow conquest of the rural provinces were the most important moments in this process. When, at the

THE HITLER YOUTH

The *Hitlerjugend* or Hitler Youth was a peripheral wing of the NSDAP designed to organize the mass of German youth. Born from the National Socialist student organization, which had great success among students in secondary schools and universities in the years of struggle against the Weimar Republic, the *Hitlerjugend* took on a precise institutional role in the Nazi Reich with a law of 1 December 1936. From this it acquired the power to mobilize into its ranks all the young people in Germany — thus achieving, under the leadership of Baldur von Schirach, head of the National Socialist student movement, a monopoly as the only permitted state youth organization, replacing the old labour and religious youth associations.

Membership of the *Hitlerjugend* became compulsory for all youths from ten to eighteen years of age, even before the organization acquired further powers in 1939. There was a separate organization for girls (the *Bund Deutscher Mädel*), affiliated to the *Hitlerjugend*, which exercised strong and exclusive political and social control as a vehicle for transmitting the ideological and cultural values of the regime. Divided into two age groups for males, from ten to fourteen (the so-called *Jungvolk*) and from fourteen to eighteen (the real *Hitlerjugend*), membership was an extension of school and covered all the free time available to young people,

involving professional as well as political processes of indoctrination. While fulfilling their sporting needs it submitted them to the demands of national militarization, turning free time into real pre-military training. The attraction of mass-orchestrated events, group entertainments and choral activities, borrowed from old traditions of the youth movement in Germany, helped the regime's penetration into the young masses. Beyond the oath of faith to the Führer which all *Hitlerjugend* members had to take, this indoctrination ensured their identification with the regime almost until the end of the war, which saw terrible sacrifices among even the youngest groups. ∎

*T*op left: a propaganda poster for the Hitlerjugend.
Below: Hitler reviews a Hitler Youth unit.
Ph. © Publiphoto

The *Bund Deutscher Mädel*, Union of German Girls, was established within the *Hitlerjugend* as a specifically female organization for German youth. While in the National Socialist Party the female element was always in a minority, conforming to the ostentatious male and virile origins of the NSDAP and reflecting the subordinate and auxiliary role given to women in National Socialist ideology, the youth movement included an increasing number of girls. At the end of 1939 the female component of the *Hitlerjugend*, with over one-and-a-half million members, was only a little smaller than the male one, which meant that about fifty per cent of members of the *Hitlerjugend* were young women. This

Top right: a "typical representative of the Aryan race" in a propaganda photo.
Below: an assembly of the Bund Deutscher Mädel *in a sports hall.*
Ph. © Publiphoto

apparent equality (merely quantitative) between males and females developed in reality into a specifically pedagogic and political organization for the recruitment and indoctrination of girls. Enlisted from the ages of ten to fourteen in *Jungmädel* groups, and from fourteen to seventeen in the *Mädel* itself, from the age of seventeen to twenty-one girls became part of the *Glaube und Schonheit* (Beauty and Fidelity) organization, founded in 1938, which accurately synthesized the function assigned to women in National Socialist ideology. The organization's programme had the sole purpose of teaching young girls their duties towards the nation, rather than towards society. They were to become mothers, according to Hitler's theories, which gave men the task of making war and supporting the government, and women essentially the role of procreating in order to secure for the nation the continuity of the race; a subsidiary role was

that of assisting men. As a symbolic reflection of the relationship of dependency on the Führer, which was eventually to become commonplace in the collective erotic imagination of the time, the inauguration ceremony in which seventeen-year-old girls entered the élitist community of Beauty and Fidelity took place annually on Hitler's birthday. A moulded woman had to emerge from the organization, capable of performing typically female tasks — a tradition already exalted in the services given by women during the First World War. This stereotypical role was necessitated by increasing collective needs in many areas, ranging from social assistance to auxiliary work: in times of war it was envisaged that women would be used both within Germany and in the occupied territories in supporting the Wehrmacht. ∎

The battle against unemployment was one of the cornerstones exploited by the NSDAP to gain popular support Below: a crowd of unemployed in front of a Berlin job centre in 1931.

beginning of 1930, the Nazis found themselves participating for the first time in a *Land* government, in Thuringia, they experimented with the political methods that later on would come to be typical features of the regime. The conquest of the *Länder* and of the most important city centres was a fundamental element in the liquidation of local autonomies and their submission under unitary control. It was not only a matter of changing the political colour of the *Länder* and the municipal administrations: it was necessary to deprive them of their functions by transferring these to local representatives of central power. This was the first step of the operation, which came to fruition with a law of 30 January 1934 which reorganized the whole structure of the Reich, abolishing every rem-

nant of power for the *Länder* and concentrating all powers in the main organs of the Reich.

Administrative districts at any level, when they were not reduced to mere geographical expressions, acquired relevance only in so far as they identified themselves with the structures of the Nazi Party. The role of the *Gauleiter*, as head of the party as well as the administrative district, derived precisely from his symbolic function as the point of convergence between political and administrative concerns and as a means of transmitting political power to the periphery. In this respect, the importance of the elimination of the federal structure in building a totalitarian state is particularly evident.

The first official photo of Hitler as the new Chancellor of the Reich, surrounded by the most important representatives of the Nazi Party: on Hitler's left can be seen Röhm, Goering, Darré, Himmler and Hess; on his right Kube, Kerrl, Goebbels and Frick (seated).
Ph. © Publiphoto

Concentration of Power Around the Führer

The establishment of the new power structure, with its concentration at the top in the person of the Führer, culminated during 1934. The process went through two distinct phases: on the one hand, the settling of accounts between diverse tendencies within the NSDAP; on the other, the ultimate definition of the role of the Führer and Chancellor of the Reich after the death of President Hindenburg. On 30 June 1934 the German public learned that a plot by the SA had been stifled; in the

armed conflict with the police and the SS, prestigious representatives of the first generation of National Socialists (including Ernst Röhm, head of the SA and at one time Hitler's close collaborator) had been killed. The bloodbath of the so-called Night of the Long Knives represented a major settling of accounts between the different components of the National Socialist movement.

However, this was not just an event within the party, but something which had more general repercussions for the structure of the new National Socialist powers. The SA had traditionally represented the active element within the NSDAP, particularly from the moment at which they had become a mass organization. An élite formation and at the same time a militant mass arranged in a military

Above: caricature showing Hitler left without enemies thanks to his guns.
Ph. © Publiphoto
Alongside: the Reichstag in plenary session in October 1930; on the left the National Socialists can be seen in the uniforms of the SA.

structure, the SA had given Hitler's party control of the streets during the years of head-on conflict, especially with regard to the labour movement. They were an authentic army which, apart from using violent methods not unlike those of the Fascist *squadrismo,* contained populist elements of the most rebellious and revolutionary type. They were the expression of a will for change, and a form of social protest. Their head, Röhm, owed his reputation above all to his military skills (he had been forced into exile for a long time for having been involved in episodes of violence against the Weimar Republic). Within the Nazi Party the SA positioned themselves as a permanent faction of violence, a sort of revolutionary armed guard, which after 30 January 1933 attempted to redefine its relationship with the conservative allies of Nazism.

Accused by outsiders of representing a real armed force in contravention of the Versailles obligations, the SA had become the protagonists of a civil war within the NSDAP. They contested the

Hitler facing the head of an SA unit during a parade; between the two can be seen Ernst Röhm, head of the SA general staff.
Ph. © Publiphoto

It has never been established exactly how many people were killed in the purge of June 1934: Hitler stated sixty-one, but there were certainly many more.
Above left: Röhm, head of the SA, shot dead in a cell in Stadelheim prison.
Above right: Gregor Strasser, head of the NSDAP political organization and leader of the party's "left". Strasser was charged with treason by Hitler because of his contacts with von Schleicher, who had offered him the post of vice-Chancellor in the formation of a new government; he was killed in Berlin on Goering's order a few hours after his arrest.
Ph. © Publiphoto

aspirations of the SS to become the central core of the regime's police and at the same time met with the hostility of the Reichswehr, which after the Nazi seizure of power considered the maintenance of an armed force of irregulars to be no longer necessary. From the point of view of the NSDAP radicals the moderate course and the stability reached at the end of 1933 fostered demands for a "second revolution", which was at odds with the need for order and normalization on the part of the Nazis in power.

The result was the repressive action with which the SS, with the support of the Reichswehr, proceeded to eliminate the general staff gathered around Röhm, who among other things was a victim of his own homosexuality and the glorification of male virtues. The "St Bartholemew's Night" of 30 June, as it was called by the exiled Nazi dissident Otto Strasser, was the occasion for Hitler to eliminate the rebellious tendencies within the NSDAP, and also liquidate the seeds of right-wing opposition in conservative circles.

Old sympathizers of the Nazis, such as ex-Chan-

THE SA STORM TROOPS

The SA (*Sturmabteilung*, or storm troops) constituted from 1921 the armed branch of the National Socialist Party. Created from the ranks to protect demonstrations and meetings of the NSDAP, it soon acquired an offensive, militant and military character comparable to Italian Fascist squads. Recruited mainly among ex-servicemen of the First World War, it was strongly anti-Bolshevik. Because of its origins and characteristics it always symbolized the soul of the NSDAP movement; for the same reasons, the SA always represented a centre of restlessness and potential conflict with the least-extremist and most politically-aware components of the NSDAP. Apart from this, the SA had a decisive influence as an attacking force within the NSDAP against its political enemies — especially after 1930, when street fighting became more bloody. At the end of 1930 the appointment as head of the SA general staff of Ernst Röhm, who had already been one of its organizers, represented a further

step towards the recognition of the SA as an auxiliary NSDAP army — an army which now contained some hundreds of thousands of armed men. After 30 January 1933 the organization was the material instrument of the first phase of aggression against the adversaries of National Socialism: it undertook the boycott and first persecution of the Jews, and was the main protagonist in the opening of the first "wild" concentration camps. Endowed by then with two million members, the SA represented an element of permanent tension inside the NSDAP, which frightened the moderate sectors and traditional supporting classes. The need to give guarantees to the moderates

Above: a provocative SA gathering in Berlin in front of the Communist Party headquarters. Below: an SA column on the march.
Ph. © Publiphoto

and especially to key groups in the armed forces, who were worried by Röhm's usurpation of a military role as the reward for his support in the seizure of power, led to Hitler's definitive settlement of accounts in the arrests and bloodbath of 30 June 1934, the first and main victim of which was Röhm. The elimination of Röhm brought not only the rebalancing of power with the Reichswehr, but also the re-evaluation of the SS and its total ascendancy over the SA, which was relegated to the secondary tasks of pre-military training. ■

cellor von Schleicher and other representatives of the Reichswehr, men of the Catholic and conservative right who might no longer be willing to back up Nazism, were eliminated along with the hard core of the SA. The NSDAP emerged more united against secessionist pressures; Himmler and the SS were strengthened. What is more, by eliminating the "alternative army" the NSDAP acquired the definite loyalty of the Reichswehr, the essential point of reference for the Nazi programmes of re-armament and military revenge.

Paradoxically, the Night of the Long Knives enlarged the moderate consensus which supported the regime. Hitler appeared to avenge and reassure those who feared the subversive shocks of Nazism in power. The death, not long after, of Hindenburg, the old president, who had perhaps unwittingly legitimized the repression, gave the ultimate definition to the power structure of the Nazis. On the eve of his death, 2 August 1934, Hindenburg agreed to proclaim the unification of the offices of Chancellor and President of the Reich in the person of Hitler.

This marked the formal completion of the power structure which made Hitler's leadership indisputable not only at the party level but now even at an institutional level. This was a detail which had enormous practical consequences and political significance: the decree signed by Hindenburg placed Hitler at the head of the armed forces, which were now obliged to take an oath of loyalty to him. With this simple signature the building of the dictatorship and the formation of the totalitarian state had taken a new and decisive step.

What is more, the *Führerprinzip*, or the principle of leadership, thus found its concrete form by moving from a merely theoretical level to an institutional level, as the foundation of the hierarchic and authoritarian character of the system. The example at the top of the Reich was to be reproduced at all levels of the political and administrative structure, establishing a precise obligation of obedience from the bottom to the top, in a hierarchical tree which culminated in the Führer. He was the charismatic leader and supreme power, synthesis and expression of the state and the national will, supreme source of law and foundation of the legitimacy of the dictatorship in both its functional and its personal aspects.

Hitler delivers a speech in an idyllic rural setting, which contrasts with the aggressiveness of his words (from a German anti-Nazi cartoon, 1933).
Below: the Apollo Theatre in Nuremberg, decorated with a huge image of Hitler for the Nazi Party congress; on Hitler's left is Julius Streicher, Gauleiter of Franconia and editor of the anti-Jewish paper Der Sturmer; on his right the mayor of Nuremberg, Liebel.
Ph. © Publiphoto

Chapter 3

REPRESSION
AND **O**BEDIENCE

THE REICH USED THE MOST DRASTIC METHODS (INCLUDING GENOCIDE) AND A POLICE APPARATUS WITH UNLIMITED POWERS AGAINST ENEMIES OF THE STATE. IT EXERCISED CONTROL AND CENSORSHIP OVER INFORMATION, CULTURE AND COLLECTIVE BEHAVIOUR, TO REDUCE THE POPULACE TO OBEDIENCE.

National Socialism wasted no time in making explicit its will to fight the enemies of the state, identified roughly as the representatives of Bolshevism, Marxism and Judaism. What was new was that this was not a conflict to be waged and resolved by political means. Since the objective was the decisive defeat and possibly the annihilation of these adversaries, the means could not be limited to propaganda or ideology alone.

Female workers salute the Reich flag before starting another day's work. The regime subdued the German people partly by means of police repression, but above all through the subordination of every manifestation of collective activity to one central influence and organization.

From the very first weeks after the seizure of power, the Nazis perfected a series of judicial instruments in a matter of a few years — between 1933 and 1936 — both organizational and institutional, which were destined both to provide legitimacy for the regime's repressive operations, and to put these repressive intentions into operation.

Even before the Reichstag fire, the way had been cleared for the arrest of presumed or real adversaries of Nazism on the basis of the simple suspicion that they might commit criminal actions against the new regime. The measures adopted after 27 February 1933 allowed for very widespread and systematic forms of persecution for precautionary reasons.

Instruments of Terror

The building of the security apparatus of the new regime was undertaken in two ways. On the one hand there was the unification of instruments of repression under a single central direction; on the other there was the politicization of the apparatus so that it became not simply a guarantor of state security but also an effective participant in the formation of a new type of state. Thus the security apparatus helped create a new type of citizen through a process either of promotion or of sackings and exclusions.

The Hindenburg decree of 28 February 1933 had already provided the judicial means of limiting and violating civil rights which had been guaranteed by the Weimar constitution. With the reform of the political police and their so-called functions of "prevention", the German citizen found himself facing an unprecedented repressive apparatus which had emerged from the liberal democratic system.

The police no longer performed the task of protecting the citizen and the state, but became a force used for repressing not just actions detri-

mental to the state or society, but simply political convictions or even a *de facto* condition (such as being Jewish), which by itself was taken as a presumption of guilt. A real perversion of the law and of the functions of the police could be useful only to a system which intended to promote change by force, by selection, and by truly violent repression. Inevitably the system immediately took on a punitive and intimidatory aspect.

The introduction of the institution of so-called protective arrest (*Schutzhaft*), in the 28 February decree, constituted the means by which the arbitrary power of the police forces could be used to eliminate anyone considered undesirable by those in power.

To arrest a person it was not necessary to possess proof, since simple suspicion was sufficient. More often, presumptions of guilt against entire categories of citizens would lead to the intervention of an increasingly autonomous police, which was more than ever the executive instrument of a political party.

It was not necessary to make any reference to the judicial authorities in order to proceed with a

Citizens of Semitic origin were the first to suffer persecution under the new regime, which among other things advocated the boycott of their commercial activities. In the photo a group of SA stands guard outside a Jewish shop, which had been shut by force. The placard reads: "Germans! Beware! Do not buy from the Jews!"

Above: *fighting between the SA and the police in 1931. Active for the first time in Munich in 1922, the SA were the most important instrument used by the Nazis to intimidate political enemies.*
Below: *the entrance to Oranienburg concentration camp in eastern Germany.*

raid against individuals considered dangerous. There was no system within which to formalize a judicial procedure. The confinement would last whatever period was considered necessary to dispel the suspicion of danger; therefore, it could last for ever. There was no punishment for this behaviour which in a constitutional state of liberal traditions would have been tantamount to illegal imprisonment. Many hundreds of thousands of people were arrested and confined in this manner in the Third Reich, as the range of individuals and groups which fell under the suspicions of the secret police widened.

Already in the first months after the seizure of power the prisoners of the regime amounted to some tens of thousands: the necessity of dealing with such a vast mass of outcasts led to the institution of concentration camps, which we will consider in more detail later. The brutality and barbarity of the methods and objectives which the Third Reich introduced with the outbreak of war then led to the ignominy of the extermination camps.

This process of purging could not have been realized without the existence of an efficient repressive apparatus. The efficiency of this apparatus derived both from its very conception and from its composition.

From the first weeks of the new regime, Hermann Goering, as the head of the new Prussian government, had promoted the reform of the old political police of the Weimar period. He took the initial steps towards its reconstruction as an autonomous organ outside the framework of the Ministry of the Interior and therefore not subjected to the latter's power of control.

Thus on 26 March 1933 the state secret police in Prussia (Gestapa; after 1936, Gestapo) was born. It would become the model for the secret police in every *Land* (now reduced to mere nominal and administrative entities).

This transformation proceeded at the local level on both a functional and a personal basis. The objective was to create a unique model for all the *Länder* which could eventually become a single instrument with jurisdiction over the whole Reich. Just as important, it would allow the fusion of the old police apparatus, once it was duly purged of officers considered incompatible with the new regime, with a loyal political staff, and guarantee for the latter effective control of the new police apparatus.

Reorganization of the Police and Security Services

The most blatant example of the process of transformation and fusion started and pursued by the regime is the case of Bavaria, where the leadership of the new political police was given to one of Hitler's closest collaborators, Heinrich Himmler, the head of the SS, who was in turn supported by his closest collaborator and head of the information service (in other words, internal espionage) of the Nazi Party, Reinhard Heydrich.

Gradually Himmler extended his powers to almost all the *Länder*, energetically and inflexibly ensuring that all posts of command were filled by men linked to the SS organization, and that the ties with the old interior administration were broken.

It has already been said that the police under the Third Reich acquired a secret and autonomous

Hitler acting as a witness at Hermann Goering's wedding on 17 March 1935. Two years earlier Goering, the head of the new Prussian government, had founded a secret police force which later, under the name of Gestapo, would exercise a pivotal role in the repression and persecution of the Reich's political enemies.

character: it became a close and despotic caste. However, the police was not a private body but one which had been assigned a public function by the state — a function which was one of the most sensitive in a modern state because it was the only appropriate way of exercising powers of coercion. Yet it is much more accurate to consider the reorganization of the police as the greatest example of the union between state and party.

From an institutional point of view, the new leadership structure of the police was finally created with the Führer's decree of 17 June 1936. On this

Munich, 9 November 1938: new SS recruits taking the oath. They would later be employed in both war manoeuvres and the supervision of extermination camps. In the foreground, just behind Hitler (speaking into the microphone), is the SS Reichsführer Heinrich Himmler. Ph. © Publiphoto

date Hitler appointed Heinrich Himmler as Reichsführer of the SS and head of the German police, the culmination of the dual process of fusing the regional police areas and the final subordination of the latter to the SS.

That the Hitler decree still talked of Himmler's function as being within the Reich Ministry of the Interior was now merely a formality; Himmler was subject to no administrative authority, as he alone exercised the office of minister and his decisions were governmental decisions.

Among other things it was important, especially in practice, that in the exercise of his powers Himmler should not be limited by any legislative obligations. As in all other Nazi legislative areas, the actual constitution was continually updated and manipulated with tactical flexibility to meet

THE SS: THE PARTY POLICE

The SS (abbreviation for *Schutzstaffen*: protection squads) were created as Hitler's bodyguard within the SA and institutionalized in 1925, on the National Socialist Party's refoundation day after the ban which followed the 1923 coup. The development of the SS into an autonomous body began in 1929, when Hitler assigned its command to Heinrich Himmler. Himmler promoted its development as a party police force, and strengthened it in numbers amongst other things (on the day of the seizure of power it was a body already numbering over 50,000 men). He aspired to turn the SS into the avant-garde of a racial aristocracy. The meticulous instructions he gave to ascertain the racial purity of SS members demonstrate his fanaticism, but also the vision of an almost monastic order, linked to the top by ties of devotion which affected even the private lives of individual members. During the war, the task of human extermination assigned to the SS pushed this blind relation of devotion and complicity to the heights of violence, almost like a psychological shield against normal inhibitions and conscience.

In fact the boundless power enjoyed by the SS — which became the largest autonomous force in the oppressive regime of the Third Reich — and through it by Himmler was due to the opportunity given to Himmler to extend his control, at the moment of the seizure of power, over the *Länder* political police. In addition their powers arose from the role they exercised in the SA repression and the murder, on 30 June 1934, of Röhm and his followers. An act by which the SS were finally released from any subjection, even formal, to the SA and were confirmed in their absolute autonomy.

Above: SS officers visit the ruins of Pompeii in Italy.
Below: a Waffen-SS sergeant is decorated with the Iron Cross.
Ph. © Publiphoto

Himmler augmented his personal power in 1936, when he became head of the German police. During the war he would accumulate other positions as well: from 1939 he was commissioner for the consolidation of the German race, which implied a leading role in the policy of genocide in the east; in August 1943 he also become the Reich Minister of the Interior, with powers second only to Hitler. However, beyond formal powers the strength of the SS lay in its control of instruments of terror: the management of the concentration camps, their economic exploitation, the acquisition of economic power with the creation of its own production activities, the setting up of its own military departments, and the Waffen-SS, which during the war became a veritable alternative army.

One must not forget that, just as the SS changed after 1933 from a party police organization into an extension of the German state, similar mutations occurred in the party security service, the so-called *Sicherheitsdienst* (SD), assigned to Reinhard Heydrich. In 1939 the SD was transformed into the Central Office for Reich Security (RSHA), destined to preside over all repressive activities and to serve as an executive body in the policy of terror and genocide. ∎

Reinhard Heydrich, head of the Central Office for Reich Security (RSHA), in the costume of a fencing master. Heydrich, appointed Reichsprotektor of Bohemia and Moravia, was assassinated while approaching the Prague Royal Palace by car on 29 May 1942.
Right: an SS soldier.

the needs of development and preservation. If there were any checks and balances, these derived exclusively from the figure of the Führer, supreme head of the executive power but also supreme source of law in the National Socialist conception of the state.

The process of incorporating the SS into the Nazi system was completed in June 1936, when Himmler reorganized the police, dividing its functions between the Public Order Police (who were charged with controlling everyday crime) and the Security Police. At the head of the Reich's security police was placed Reinhard Heydrich, who thus became the head of the Reich's central security mechanism.

On 27 September 1939 Reinhard Heydrich's role was further enhanced, when the central security police and the SS security service were officially merged into the Reichssicherheits-Hauptampt (RSHA), which was not given an executive function, but rather an information and research role in the identification and elimination of the enemies of the Reich.

With the outbreak of the world war and the ensuing persecutions and exterminations, the SD and the RSHA increasingly extended the scope of their activity outside of the information and theory fields, to prepare the broad outlines and the specific projects designed to implement the extermination operations of the Third Reich.

It is superfluous to remind the reader of the role of the SD special groups (the *Einsatzgruppen*) in political and racial extermination operations in the occupied territories in the East, starting with the invasion of Poland, or of the role played by Section IV of the RSHA under the leadership of Adolf Eichmann in planning the completion of the so-called "final solution" — that is, the genocide of the Jews in all areas of Europe occupied by the Wehrmacht.

Below: Nazi propaganda in schools. The indoctrination of young people in the schoolroom was part of the disciplinary process. However, in Mein Kampf *Hitler had already announced that education in the Third Reich would be conducted principally through spartan training for a life based on compulsory work and military activity.*

The Establishment of Cultural Uniformity

The tactics of intimidation by which the new regime sought to subordinate large masses into obedience and passivity were partly carried out through this repressive apparatus, but even more so through channels of collective discipline. Information, culture and every type of human expression and behaviour was controlled by one central influence and organization.

Apart from the permanent threat of the concentration camps, the state pursued a policy specifically aimed at establishing, even in spiritual and intellectual fields, a real *Gleichschaltung* (uniformity) of culture, which assumed an obedience as planned and comprehensive as possible. The Nazi regime made shrewd use of mass media, which had largely been developed in Germany during the First World War for war propaganda. It also utilized the assault strategy of mass campaigns, laden with charm as well as sinister threats, almost as if they were a new form of primitive ritual, in which the collective identity of the population was cemented with the arguments and symbols of

National Socialism. At the start of the new regime the German population, whose traditional values had been undermined by the 1919 institutional change and the wounds left by the crisis in the economy, was asked to rediscover its own identity through the condemnation of presumed enemies and through exciting but ultimately self-defeating acts of violence.

The burning of banned books on 10 May 1933 was not a spontaneous and untrammelled explosion of popular anger: it was an operation consciously controlled by young academics — not just students — and those responsible for the Reich's propaganda. It was intended to create a sense of general tension to make people accept, without any reservation, the symbolic destruction of the enemy and his responsibility for Germany's evils. The book burning was also to assist in the processes of popular cohesion to help legitimize the actions of the Reich's new government and facilitate consensus for its directives.

The creation and diffusion of state propaganda were among the relatively new events which followed the establishment of the Nazi regime. They reflected all Hitler's ideas on the possibilities and necessity of manipulating the masses which had matured over the years of his political apprenticeship — and collected in *Mein Kampf* — as well as the experience of a strategic expert in propaganda in the form of his collaborator Joseph Goebbels, who saw in the freedom of the press in the Weimar period and in the great development of the democratic Press, one of the main obstacles to the affirmation of Nazism.

A *painting by George Grosz: Café (1918–19). The artist, representative of the Berlin avant-garde, was among those most persecuted by the new regime. Already tried and sentenced for obscenity and blasphemy during the Weimar period, he emigrated to the United States in 1931 and remained there until 1959.*

His hatred for the strong pacifist and anti-nationalist political journalism of those years was certainly the origin of operations like the burning of banned literature, which was meant to signify refusal of and contempt for the values that the Press and literature professed. But in general his attack was against all trends of modern thought, not only avant-garde art, but also psychoanalysis and the theory of relativity, not only Marxism but also the "Frankfurt school", Dada, abstractionism and twentieth century music, from American Jazz

(including the tradition of black music) to the Vienna school.

On 11 March 1933, Joseph Goebbels was given responsibility for a new department of popular culture and propaganda, an institution which

had a precedent in the activities of the Nazi Party in Thuringia in 1930 and which would be reproduced by the Italian Fascist regime in 1934. The creation of such a ministry indicated a definite policy: the determination to create a centralized system for information and the formation of public opinion, to the point of making the very concept of public opinion debatable. It also revealed its aim of bringing every artistic and cultural manifestation within the sole allowable model, reducing or reversing the very role of intellectuals, who from being champions of political and cultural debate in the Weimar period, critics of democracy and heroes of the democratization of German society, were now forced to become the mouthpieces of the regime or stay silent.

Josef Goebbels (centre), the Reich Minister for Culture and Propaganda, with two film actors approved of by the regime.

Persecution of Intellectuals

The first result of this Nazi policy was the expulsion of thousands of intellectuals, artists, academics and scientists, who were forced to flee Germany for political and racial reasons. The regime made a great show of the lists of proscribed persons as if they were bulletins of victories on the battlefields, but the actual reality was the impoverishment of cultural life, not from a quantitative point of view, but from a qualitative one.

The best representatives of German culture found themselves forced to work abroad, in neighbouring European countries, and later on in America. Many masterpieces of German litera-

Anti-Nazi emigration was a much more striking phenomenon than any internal opposition to the regime. Thousands of intellectuals, men and women of culture and science, and show-business personalities left Nazi Germany, either voluntarily or under the direct threat of persecution. This exodus began in the first weeks of Hitler's domination, anticipating the measures for "denial of citizenship" which the Nazi government initiated in August 1933. This type of emigration (it would be better to call it exile, as was pointed out by, among others, Bertolt Brecht, in a well-known poem) was followed in subsequent years by waves of those who emigrated to escape racial persecution — a real mass emigration — and a debilitating flow of intellectuals and scientists from Austria

(among them Freud and Robert Musil) after its annexation to the Reich. The main destinations for émigrés were at first Third Republic France, and Benes' liberal and tolerant Czechoslovakia. But pressure after the 1939 German invasions turned the destiny of many migrants into tragedy, as they were forced to search for new lands. The most fortunate reached England and the

United States (where a large colony of exiles, including Heinrich and Thomas Mann, was already established before the war, the less successful fell prisoner to the German forces. Many committed suicide, either from fear of falling in the hands of the Nazis (Walter Benjamin, among others) or became victims of existential despair in an age when it seemed that nothing could stop Nazism (Ernst Toller and others).

The migrants continued to live and work in new contexts, disseminating their cultural and linguistic wealth and allowing a new cultural osmosis between Europe and America, which was particularly evident in the grafting of the Frankfurt School onto the US social science tradition. Hollywood cinema and American music also enjoyed the benefits of a strong interchange with artists and performers coming from Central Europe. Rather than preparing for any return to Germany, the mission of the émigrés was to denounce the nature and crimes of Nazism and Fascism — hence their almost unanimous condemnation of the Spanish Civil War. ■

*T*wo writers hated by the regime: above, Bertolt Brecht (seated); left, Alfred Döblin. Both left Germany.

ture, by Thomas and Heinrich Mann, by Brecht and many other authors, were created outside Germany.

For twelve years the directives of Goebbels's policy gave the German public no opportunity to look at contemporary art: Germans were obliged to see only the products of German art — not the freely-produced works which had characterized the

A painting by Emil Nolde: The Admirer *(1919). An eminent representative of the expressionist movement, Nolde was expelled from the Arts Academy and forbidden to paint. During the regime's campaign against so-called "degenerate art", 1,052 of his works exhibited in German museums were confiscated. Unlike other artists opposed by Nazism, Nolde continued to proclaim himself a fervent patriot, but his declarations of faith towards Germany did not stop him being ostracized.*

high cultural level of the Weimar years, but those considered typically German by the Nazi regime. These consisted of any celebratory sort of painting, monumental and representative architecture, rhetorical and militaristic music, and cinema which was inspired by past and future military grandeur or aggressive anti-Semitism.

The creation on 15 November 1933 of the

Reich Cultural Chamber, under Goebbels's presidency unified all cultural and professional specializations into one centre of inspiration upon which they were all dependent. This represented at an institutional level the culmination of the process of fusing powers of control. Nobody who was not a member of the Cultural Chamber could work at any activity which fell within its area of control. The

Left: a painting by Karl Schmidt-Rottluff: Landscape in Dangast *(1910). Among the founders of the* Die Brücke *group, Schmidt-Rottluff — like all the exponents of expressionism — was persecuted by the regime, but he did not leave Germany. Below: the composer Arnold Schoenberg portrayed by Egon Schiele. Leader of a "degenerate" artistic movement, Schoenberg had dared to subvert the traditional values of tonality and, above all, was of Jewish origin (though he had converted to Protestantism). Schoenberg emigrated to Paris — where as a protest against Nazism he reconverted to Judaism — and later to the United States.*

Chamber had a monopoly in the labour market in those specified sectors, and also the monopoly of control on the quality of activities and events. In fact it exercised a real censorship, comparable to that exercised over the press by Goebbels in his ministerial role, but in this instance over individuals or individual events or the publication of books.

The autonomy of the artists who were left in Germany proved to be very limited. The majority of those who did not fall within the aesthetic ideals of the regime were condemned to silence: Barlach and Kollwitz stopped giving exhibitions, as did Schmidt-Rottluff and other big names of the Twenties. The

Munich, 11 July 1938: Hitler and other officials watch a procession depicting "Two thousand years of German civilization" during German Art Day.
Ph. © Publiphoto
Below: Nuremberg stadium (an Albert Speer project, 1934).

music of Felix Mendelssohn and Gustav Mahler was banned as Jews' work, while Schoenberg was defamed both as a Jew and as the destroyer of tonality.

From June 1937, in the new Munich Cultural Centre (*Haus der Kunst*), a neo-classical building designed by one of the regime's architects, the public was offered an annual exhibition of the great works of German art. These consisted exclusively of figurative paintings and sculptures, productions of a conformist and provincial system, such as pseudorealist photographic nudes, peasant scenes, family groups with blue eyes and blonde hair, portraits of the Führer, of soldiers and military leaders, of workers at work, and of the regime's works.

In July of the same year, 1937, a "degenerate art" exhibition was designed to ridicule the twentieth-century avant-garde, starting with the fashionable, typically German expressionism.

The condemnation of "cultural Bolshevism" and of the "Jewish pollution" of experimental and avant-garde art did not simply involve the disappearance from public view of thousands of art works, which were removed from museums. Apart from a few dozen works sold abroad in order to obtain valuable currency, thousands were burned. Nazi denunciation was manifested not only in

ostracism, but in the physical destruction of a substantial number of art works with a symbolic violence which often evoked the ghost of iconoclasm. It was an operation without precedent in the twentieth century but one that would be repeated in occupied countries after the beginning of the Second World War.

These mass campaigns were aided by the energetic use of the radio as a means of communication — a privileged communication medium, moreover, for the Führer. Great set-piece parades and gatherings of the National Socialist Party (in particular on the occasion of the annual Nuremberg rallies) gave the appearance of power and order which represented the overthrow of the Weimar chaos and the return to national and racial values.

In its own way, the "Night of Broken Glass" on 9 November 1938 was also a symbol of an ordered and homogenous society, with perfect symmetries, without diversity. This image corresponded to the reality

1934: the première of Triumph of the Will, *a film about the Nazi Party congress which Hitler commissioned from the director Leni Riefenstahl. Ph. © Publiphoto Below: Leni Riefenstahl.*

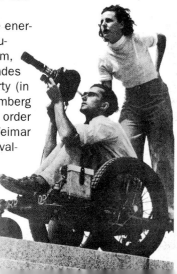

of a society that permited prohibition, exclusion and intimidation, and could increasingly restrain the scope for autonomy and alternative views.

Even the area of religious beliefs was restrained, though with some more or less favourable and respectable compromises. A Concordat with the Catholic Church on 30 June 1933 marked a moment of great prestige for the regime, which viewed the Concordat as its first recognition by an international authority of high moral value. German Catholicism was forced to obedience or passivity. It had a few moments of dignified reaction (mainly against euthanasia) on the part of a few people with consciences, but this was its sole

NAZISM AND

Within the Third Reich the Churches' role was determined by the regime's need to isolate possible centres of autonomy and opposition, and to exploit instead their moral and social influence in order to consolidate a consensus for its own purposes.

The major task was to align German Protestantism, the religion of the majority, to the new regime, encouraging the *Deutsche Christen* organization (to which about one-fifth of clergymen adhered) to be in favour of the union between Nazism and Christianity — to the point of accepting the persecution of the Jews. After the reform of the constitution of the German Evangelical Church in July 1933, the regime supported the election of a Reich bishop, in the person of Ludwig Müller. They failed, however, to break the opposition of a substantial

core of evangelist clergy gathered around the Confessional Church, inspired by Karl Barth's theology and animated by the example of Martin Niemöller and other clergymen. The refusal to apply the so-called *Arierparagraph* (Aryan paragraph) among evangelist clergy represented the deepest theological and political motive for a schism in German Protestantism, which produced highly valued ethical figures (such as Bonhoeffer). However, externally the Evangelic Church maintained (as did the Catholic Church) an attitude of total acquiescence towards the regime, never publicly distancing itself from it. Relations with the Catholic Church were more complex, as they involved the Vatican. In the first months of Nazi domination the German clergy and the Holy See supported an agreement which would become known as the Concordat. Signed on 20 July

1933 by the Catholic vice-Chancellor von Papen and Cardinal Pacelli, in the hope of protecting the Catholic Church from interference by the regime, it offered in exchange the elimination of Catholic political organizations and a commitment to steer clear of political life.

In reality, the idea of the Church maintaining influence over Catholic associations and schools was soon thwarted. The creation in 1935 of a specific Reich Ministry for Religious Affairs indicated the end of the policy of caution pursued up to then by Hitler. It followed an anti-Church offensive by the regime (imprisonment of clergymen, sequestration of goods, and limits to the activities of monasteries and religious bodies), which culminated in the exacerbation of racist policy after the publication of the encyclical *Mit brennender Sorge* in March 1937. In this defence against the triumph of Nazism. The position of Protestantism was more compromised: with the exception of a few brave clergymen and lay people of the Confessional Church (*Bekennende Kirche*), the tradition of loyalty to the government and solidarity to nationalism typical of German Protestantism prevented any dissidence from the institutional Church. Protestantism was the religion of consensus or passivity towards the regime, which formally respected the Church's autonomy, but which in actual fact had been able to neutralize its independence and exploit its support or its silence.

The signing of the Concordat between the Holy See and Nazi Germany in July 1933. From left: the prelate Kaas, vice-Chancellor von Papen, Vatican Secretary of State Cardinal Eugenio Pacelli (in the process of signing), Buttmann (an official of the Ministry of the Interior), and the embassy official Klee. On the right, standing, is Cardinal Montini (the future Pope Paul VI).
Ph. © Publiphoto

THE CHURCHES

Pope Pius XI, without denouncing Nazi racism and anti-Semitism altogether, attacked its doctrinal aspects as heralding a new paganism. The German Church did not take matters further, leaving its individual representatives, notably the Bishop of Berlin, von Preysing, and von Galen, Bishop of Munster, with the freedom to denounce the crimes of the regime (von Galen proclaimed himself officially against euthanasia) and then be subjected to retaliation in the form of persecution. The Nazi anti-Bolshevik crusade removed any potential reservations and prevented the dissension of individuals from encouraging the Church as a whole to take a stand. ■

ALLE ZEHNJÄHRIGEN IN DIE HJ.

NAZI PROPAGANDA USED THE CONCEPT OF "POPULAR COMMUNITY" TO CONSOLIDATE COLLECTIVE DISCIPLINE AND JUSTIFY RACIAL DISCRIMINATION. WITH THE NUREMBERG LAWS, JEWS BEGAN TO BE LEGALLY AND SYSTEMATICALLY PERSECUTED IN A VIOLENT CLIMATE WHICH WOULD END WITH THE "NIGHT OF THE BROKEN GLASS".

The keyword "popular community" (*Volksgemeinschaft*), a glorified expression describing all those belonging to the national society in Nazi terminology, was used with a variety of meanings. It is possible to identify at least three types of circumstances in which the expression acquired a strong significance. There were a number of real and ideological matters which came together to create the *Volksgemeinschaft*.

The ideology of "popular community" served in the first place to represent the position of classes in society, and the very structure of the social pyramid theorized by the Third Reich. It delineated in other ways, through the definite opposition between the insiders and outsiders of the popular community, the judicial level of citizenship: between those who had access to services, rights and privileges, and those excluded. Finally, it acquired a racist meaning, which was, in some ways, a point of synthesis at the social and legal level, in the sense that social and judicial hierarchies identified themselves with a precise hierarchy of races, as something which excluded every other notion of belonging. This was a simplifying element but also, implicitly, an extremely complex one.

A poster invites German boys to join the Hitler Youth. The picture shows a boy with the typical features of what was considered the "select race", German and Aryan, belonging to which was an essential prerequisite to being considered a member of the Reich "popular community".
Ph. © Publiphoto

Racial and Social Hierarchies

From a social perspective, the first observation one can make about the concept of "popular community" is that it had a corporatist nature. It was

Above: poster acclaiming the return of the Saar to Germany, achieved unanimously on 7 March 1935. The claim to lost territories inhabited by German-speaking peoples was inspired by ideals designed to bring about a Greater Germany. Right: advertisement for Volkswagen automobiles, the people's means of transport, which every German could afford by saving "five marks each week".

apparently aimed at breaking down every division between classes, carefully avoiding any terminology which would confirm its existence. The ideology of popular community asserted a fictitious equality between classes and all components of society. But equality was denied at the very point at which the division of labour reappeared in the definition of roles in society, and with it the articulation of a hierarchically-structured society. Equality lay only in the fact that all employers and workers had to be *Volksganossen,* part of the same race; but within this basic structure there was not to be any confusion between those who held the power of command and those whose only role was to obey.

From a political and social perspective, the ideological deception accomplished by the regime was of great importance. The call for collective membership of the popular community was a very strong incentive to the consolidation of discipline and the development of collective sanctions. Through this sense of belonging the regime established consensus: the acceptance not only of established hierarchies, but also of the tasks and functions which the regime had set itself as goals. This was illusory, signifying that all those belonging to the community would participate in its destiny, if not in its decision-making. But it represented a force for the homogenization of behaviour which seemed to validate the regime's belief in the existence of a society without conflict, a community, and which emphasized the people's ability to discipline themselves.

Propaganda poster underlining the spirit of unity between people from different generations and with different tasks and responsibilities in Hitler's Germany.

The regime's propaganda relied in the most basic and also the most deceptive way on the contrast between the chaos of the Weimar period and the absence of conflict after 1933, with the falling unemployment that resulted from rearmament. There is no doubt, however, that the sense of cohesion sought in this immense exercise in collective discipline yielded some positive results — and not only as a result of propaganda, but also because of the development of a concrete social policy. This can be seen in the acquiescence with which the working classes accepted the developments which would lead to the outbreak of war. In addition, during the years of conflict it guaranteed high levels of arms production without the dissent which might have jeopardized efficiency.

The delineation of the popular community was particularly effective with regard to those who were bound to remain excluded from it. These were not second-class citizens, or even enemies, but all sorts of groups which were potentially identified as "outcasts", destined to be excluded from all rights and subjected to discrimination, in the sense that they could perform only those functions which would benefit the popular community; in the most extreme cases, these outcasts were doomed to be physically eliminated. At a later point we will return to the subject of the segregating institutions of the Third Reich, and especially the concentration camp system. It is interesting here, however, to note that the large groupings outside the popular community were not simply composed of those who passively observed the doings of the more privileged strata of society. These groupings were, with a few exceptions, also destined to be involved in the process

A lorry with a poster ridiculing the presumed "enemies" of Germany: those refusing sterilization, the great landowners, an Aryan girl dancing with a Jew, a licentious young man, a nun collecting money. The poster reads: "We will not tolerate any sabotage of the Führer's work!".

of mobilization, although of a different nature from that of those belonging to the popular community.

In addition to the Jews and other marginal groups whose very manual labour was rejected, this category also included foreign workers and, after the invasion of Europe, the great mass of deported forced labourers and others originating from the occupied territories. Those destined for concentration camps, including so-called "asocial" persons, were comparable to those outside the popular community because of racial origin, nationality, and social and cultural origin. In order to consolidate the homogeneity of the popular community, the discrimination to which all the outcasts were subjected was not by itself important: more significant was the sense of security which was created. The outcasts, excluded from the equality (artificial as it was) of the popular community, became the recipients of all social tensions — from which the *Volksgemeinschaft* was protected.

In the collective imagination, there were individuals outside the popular community who were, in one way or another, liable to spoil the symmetry of the hierarchic order created by the regime, or to have no place in the hierarchic scheme (the Jews, for example) or, still worse, to demonstrate in their behaviour the breaking of rules and the transgression of customs and conventions. Mechanisms of exclusion were established beyond judicial boundaries, deeply embedded in the psychology of the majority who adopted violence towards and persecution of the excluded — which were rendered more brutal as more and more people identified with a political and ethical imperative.

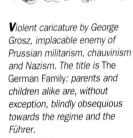

Violent caricature by George Grosz, implacable enemy of Prussian militarism, chauvinism and Nazism. The title is The German Family: *parents and children alike are, without exception, blindly obsequious towards the regime and the Führer.*
Ph. © Publiphoto

In simple terms the very fact of being inside or outside the popular community was translated into a contrast between those who were good and those who were bad, between Good and Evil, concepts linked as ever to the racial ideas which were the basis of the popular community. Those who were outside were excluded for being part of an inferior race, or for not belonging to the superior race. In this way the concept of "popular community" served to designate the supremacy of the racially pure and the socially accountable, who determined the access of all who wanted to belong to the community.

The relationship between social accountability and racial quality was a very close one, in the

sense that the acquisition of higher social status was possible only within the select race, with an almost biological identification between professional abilities and racial features. It was thus assumed that according to the leadership principle, the *Führerprinzip,* from which the whole pyramid of social and racial hierarchy descended from top to bottom, those at the top embodied the best capabilities and the highest human and moral values, not according to a social and cultural selection, but precisely as a result of superior racial quality. The racial element was therefore the primary consideration.

Above: German propaganda poster against the Jews and the Allies: "Behind the enemy powers, the Jews".
Below: Nazi militants demonstrate with posters warning Germans against the Jews.

The Nuremberg Race Laws

We have already mentioned the anti-Semitic tradition and the tenacity with which the NSDAP made anti-Semitism one of the cornerstones of its political rise: the key element of consensus around which its programme was created. The Nazis in power set about creating detailed legislation and a long series of administrative provisions to establish judicial discrimination against the German Jew — no longer only social and cultural discrimination, as had been the case in the past. Until the outbreak of the Second World War, discriminatory

activity mainly had the objective of compelling the Jews to emigrate, leaving Germany and abandoning their wealth. After this proved ineffective, the provisions against the Jewish population acquired an increasingly oppressive character, culminating in their increasingly violent segregation and even their physical destruction.

When on 15 September 1935 Hitler announced in Nuremberg the two key laws which would codify the new constitution for Jews, the regime already had in place a substantial array of provisions against the Jews, which constituted a solid base for the limitation of their legal rights. With the law of 7 April 1933 on the purge of public administration, it had been possible to get rid of officers of "non-Aryan origin" (a description of those with at least one Jewish grandparent). With successive decrees Jews were expelled from other professions, from the judiciary to medicine and dentistry.

In April 1933 quotas were introduced to control Jewish access to schools and universities. In May the Jews were banned from being financial consultants. In July all citizenships acquired by Jews between 9 November 1918 and 1933 were revoked. On 29 September 1933 a law on the inheritance of

Above: poster for the anti-Semitic movie Der Ewige Jude *(The Jewish Peril), directed by Fritz Hippler (1940).*
Below: illustration in a children's book showing children reading pages from the anti-Semitic newspaper Der Sturmer, *edited by Julius Streicher.*

*A*bove: Hitler attending a
concert with Goebbels and his
wife.
Ph. © Publiphoto
Right: Alfred Rosenberg,
considered the "intellectual
leader" of the Nazi Party, whose
hatred for Jews and Bolsheviks
was praised by Hitler. Below:
front page of Der Sturmer with a
cartoon showing how the Jews
were planning to exterminate all
non-Jewish people.

land made it essential not to have "Jewish blood" in order to inherit real estate. Not being of Jewish origin became the preliminary condition for access to professional training in almost all fields, included the military.

With the creation of the Reich Cultural Chamber, Jews were excluded from cultural activities open to the general public. However, typical of a segregated and isolated society, they were granted the right to enjoy separate cultural activities designated specifically for their own race. Then came the creation of a federation of Jewish cultural associations, placed under the supervision of Goebbels's ministry, which until the first years of the war — that is, while this type of activity was actually allowed — was responsible for a very rich vein of performances in theatrical and musical fields, as well as editorial and film initiatives. The Jews were also excluded from sporting activities, which could be enjoyed only in so far as they were promoted separately and concerned events conducted exclusively between Jews and watched exclusively by Jews. What is more, from the first weeks of Nazi power the Jews' commercial activities had been subject to a NSDAP boycott; a boycott which moved and spread beyond the field of commercial activity in the strict sense. It was a form of social discrimination against Jews, for whom the state no longer guaranteed any protection: Jews were no longer citizens with equal rights even before the Nuremberg laws.

An SS group affixing posters on the window of a Jewish shop in Bayreuth in the early 1930s, warning German people not to shop there.

And yet the Nuremberg laws affected their legal position in a fundamental way. There were two legislative provisions: a law on Reich citizenship; and a law for the protection of German blood and honour. The former decreed that only people of German or similar racial origin could be citizens of the Reich — that is, citizens with a full range of political rights. Consequently "a Jew cannot be a citizen of the Reich. He does not enjoy any right to vote on political issues; he cannot fill any public office." The law on citizenship no longer left loopholes, not even for Jews who had fought during the First World War, as had been the case until then. The law on the protection of German blood banned, in the interests "of the preservation of the German people", marriage between Jews and citizens of German blood and annulled those which had already taken place. It ruled out sexual relations between the two groups, on pain of imprisonment and other punishments for transgressors. Particularly contemptible were the provisions by which the Jews were denied the right to employ "citizens of German or similar blood under the age of forty-five" as domestic servants, or to fly the Reich's flag.

Apart from the effects of specific decrees, the Nuremberg laws had psychological, political and judicial significance. From a psychological point of view, the codification and dissemination of discrimination broke all barriers and removed all inhibitions; anti-Semitism was not only something normal and legal, but it was also something compulsory. In effect, the biological (and not merely cultural) character of Nazi racism was rendered even more rigid and widespread by the implementation of the Nuremberg laws and the consequent construction of family trees designed to test the

Nuremberg, 1938: Hitler at the Nazi Party congress, carrying the sacred "flag of blood" (stained with the blood of the victims of the failed Munich putsch of 1923). In his congress speech the Führer boasted that he would not tolerate "further oppression of those of the German race living in Czechoslovakia", and claimed for the German-speaking people of that country the right to the self-determination "which every people possesses for itself".
Ph. © Publiphoto

Jewish or Aryan origins of those under scrutiny.

The denial of full citizenship to the Jews — who, incidentally, had not been declared formally stateless — created strong pressure for their expatriation with the abandonment of their possessions. But above all, once the Jews had been completely separated from the rest of the German population there were no longer any ties of common destiny, and thus the possibility of acts of solidarity towards the Jews was reduced. The profile of the Jews diminished, in the sense that, once they had been segregated and officially and publicly defamed — not for what they did against the regime but for what they were, simply because they existed — they could be subjected to any oppression without it creating much commotion. From 1 January 1939, the identity documents of every Jew had to contain a new first name: Israel for males and Sarah for females.

And yet the process of separating Jews from the rest of German society was only just beginning.

The Night of Broken Glass: From Discrimination to Pogrom

During 1938 the persecution of the Jews came to a new head. First of all, the Jewish population

within the Reich had increased. With the Austrian *Anschluss* in March the Third Reich had absorbed 200,000 more Jews within its boundaries, mostly in Vienna — which had already seen the development of an entrenched anti-Semitic movement. Local collaboration and the zeal of an SS specialist, Adolf Eichmann, who was sent to Vienna to speed up the expatriation of Austrian Jews, allowed the implementation of new and sophisticated techniques for the expulsion of Jews and the expropriation of their property.

The techniques used in Austria to sequestrate Jewish property to the advantage of the Nazi Party became increasingly widespread in a process that was now called the "Aryanization" of Jewish property. In fact this amounted to a policy of robbery, expropriation and, at the very least, the selling off of goods and possessions belonging to Jews. A register of Jewish property, decreed in April 1938,

Above: the Austrian Anschluss — the Germans arrive in Salzburg.
Ph. © Publiphoto
Left: cartoon showing Jews persecuted by the Nazis in all countries.

was the prelude to its final confiscation for the benefit of the German economy — especially the war economy. By the following June and July the point was reached when Jews were banned from the exercise of most commercial activities.

The complete exclusion of Jews from economic life became in this period the main policy of Marshal Goering, as the person in charge of the Four-Year Plan — a programme of economic preparation for war. It was a policy which, apart from the value of the actual properties which were sequestrated, had a demagogic and disrupting impact. It was almost like seeking mass approval to legitimize this final act of a series of depredations which had been going on for years, as well as consensus for preparation for war.

The Munich Treaty of 30 September 1938, in which Western democracy at the height of its policy of appeasement agreed to sacrifice Czechoslovakia to the Third Reich, under the illusion that this concession would stop Nazi territorial expansion, did not placate but galvanized and accelerated the persecution of the Jews.

The *Kristallnacht* on 9 November was not spontaneous: it was the culmination of a series of provo-

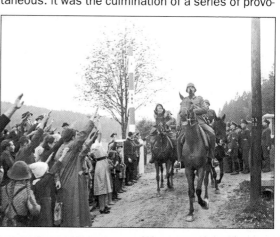

Above: portrait of a young Hermann Goering, national hero of the First World War and a member of the Nazi Party since 1921.
Right: the population of the Sudetenland welcome with jubilation the arrival the first German soldiers, commanded by Colonel Ritten von Loeb, in 1938.
Ph. © Publiphoto

cations. The immediate occasion for the outburst of violence was a decree issued at the end of October ordering the expulsion from the Reich of Jews of Polish citizenship, many of whom had lived there for generations. On 7 November a young Polish emigrant killed a senior officer of the German embassy in Paris as a protest against the deportation of his parents from the Reich. During the night of 9–10 November Germany was struck by the most awful wave of anti-Semitic violence that Europe had seen since the time of the Tsarist pogroms.

Hundreds of synagogues were set on fire, thousands of shops and offices belonging to the Jews were destroyed, houses were torched, many Jews were attacked and a few dozen were killed. Thousands were arrested and deported to concentration camps. But it was not a spontaneous reaction of the German population, united against an international Jewish plot to overthrow Germany, as Nazi propaganda held it to be. It was one of the mass campaigns promoted and manoeuvred by Goebbels, who was in charge of education and propaganda and who, in fact, authorized the NSDAP and the SA to unleash the pogrom.

A synagogue burning in Berlin in 1938.

How and why did they do it at that precise moment? What were the reasons for staging an intimidatory operation of doubtful propaganda appeal to the outside world, which was still trying to digest the Munich appeasement? One might think that the Nazis wanted to stage a show of force as a provocative gesture towards international public opinion, a demonstration that they would not retreat before any obstacle. It is more

A scene of daily life in Berlin in 1939: people standing quietly in the square in front of the Reich Chancellery, seemingly unaware of the dramatic events which were to come.
Ph. © Publiphoto
Below: the first Jewish refugee children from Germany, Austria and the Sudetenland arrive in London in December 1938.

likely that it was an internal operation designed to complete a *Gleichschaltung,* a numbing of consciences and public opinion, in order to discourage any residual dissidence. If that was the intention, it was achieved.

Many shocked and confused Germans witnessed this new iconoclastic wave, except that now it was not only paintings that were being destroyed but human lives. There was no public reaction. The Jews, totally isolated in society, were forced to pay a very harsh price as a consequence of the event. The Aryanization of Jewish wealth was further accelerated and the Nazi leaders discussed the possibility of confining Jews in ghettos and eventually obliging them to wear a distinguishing sign. Restrictions on movement began to proliferate, as did bans on attendance at public entertainments. All Jews were banned from schools and universities, all Jewish firms were closed and all Jewish funds were expropriated. Jewish driving licences were withdrawn; Jews were forced to forfeit all their gold and jewels; rents for Jews were increased. A system of Jewish residential ghettos was established, and at the outbreak of the war a curfew was imposed on them.

The war led, if anything, to an increased number of provisions against Jews, in an atmosphere of contempt and sadism. Jews, depicted in propaganda as the enemy, became the enemy in living reality. All radios were seized from Jews (29 September 1939), regardless of whether or not they listened to enemy broadcasts. Ration cards for clothes and fuel were not issued to Jews (6 February 1940). Jews in Berlin could only buy food between four and five in the afternoon (4 July 1940), so that they did not contaminate the shopping public with their presence. The obligatory wearing of the yellow star within the Reich (9 September 1941) followed, as an external sign of the Jews' status as enemies, a symbol of their demonization. This mirrored what was already happening in the occupied territories. From that moment on there was no obstacle to hinder the final settling of accounts with the Jews, as Nazi leaders had threatened before the war.

On the night of 9 November 1938 the last traces of inhibition were erased.

Before the closure of the frontier, the remaining German citizens living in Poland moved, with considerable difficulty, to the Reich.
Ph. © Publiphoto

Chapter 5

THE **O**RGANIZATION OF
LABOUR AND **R**EARMAMENT

THE SUBSTANTIAL FALL IN UNEMPLOYMENT CONCEALED THE REALITY OF AN ECONOMY ONLY REVITALIZED THROUGH MILITARY EXPENDITURE. WHILE THE INDUSTRIAL GROUPS AND STATE HOLDINGS FOCUSED ON REARMAMENT, THE LABOUR FRONT WAS ABLE TO SECURE THE CONSENSUS OF MILLIONS OF WORKERS.

T he German working class had suffered a double defeat in the 1930s: it was hit by the economic crisis which fractured its unity and its ability to defend its interests and fight; and it was further targeted by the Nazis, who deliberately aimed to destroy what remained of its organization, and especially to deprive the trade union movement of its functions as a representative and protector of workers. Just as it could not tolerate a plurality of political parties, the Nazi regime could not allow autonomous workers' organizations either.

The concept of society as a popular community, where race and nation represented at the same time the synthesis and the replacement of all other values, involved the rejection of social and political pluralism. In essence, free unions were a contradiction within a system like that of the Nazis — which, by assuming the fusion of a social consensus around the objectives of internal cohesion and the external expansion of the Third Reich, could not tolerate forces which did not revolve around the same objectives, and therefore could not accept the principle of free collective bargaining on either wages or working conditions.

German rearmament, decided upon personally by Hitler after his appointment as Chancellor of the Reich, was a key element in the recovery of the German economy and the fall of unemployment, which in 1933 had reached five million; the war industry strengthened support for the regime on the part of the armed forces and industry, interested in public spending. Opposite: a German anti-aircraft gun during the Second World War.

Berlin: picketing in front of the underground entrance during a strike by public transport workers in November 1932; within a few months the right to strike would be abolished.
Below: a group of young people entering a camp run by the Labour Front, an organization which also provided them with paramilitary training.
Ph. © Publiphoto

Ultimately, the need to impose political control upon a social group like the working class was one of the imperatives which contributed to the creation of organizational and disciplinary measures aimed at removing every form of autonomy and individuality from the organized working class.

The Working Class under the Third Reich

The forced dissolution of free trade unions and the confiscation of their property (a huge fortune, which was to a great extent linked with the recreational and cultural activities of the free associations) took place on 2 May 1933, coinciding significantly with the traditional workers' holiday, which became in Nazi parlance the national day of work. On the following 10 May the *Deutsche Arbeitsfront*, the German Labour Front, was founded as an organization in which workers, employees and employers enjoyed a nominal and formal role as equal partners. In reality it was merely another glorified aspect of the popular community, nothing like a trade union organization.

As a specialized wing of the National Socialist Party, the role of the German Labour Front was firstly to extend the party's ideological control beyond the area of its direct influence; and sec-

ondly to function as part of the great machine of social consensus, controlling a wide range of initiatives relating to the use of free time and all workers' recreational activities, subjecting these to propaganda and to the regime's general objectives. All these organizational measures were to assume an even more rigid character, providing further essential support for the system, as the demands of the war necessitated the increasing and more thorough exploitation of working people.

From a body for collective organization, the Labour Front thus developed into a vehicle for mobilization for war. Nevertheless it also played a role in protecting some of the interests of German workers (that is, of those participating in the popular community, often in opposition to foreign workers), without ever being able to influence wage policy. But the opportunities it did have to act — through the provision of social security and the improvement of conditions — were part of its institutional role in the policy of building consensus around the regime.

Through the Labour Front, as the most important mass organization in the Third Reich, were channelled huge collective campaigns, such as those for "winter aid", demagogic messages and the reassuring activities of the *Kraft durch Freude*

*P*ropaganda poster for the afterwork organization Kraft Durch Freude, *showing a new agricultural colony. Below: the Labour Front Congress on 10 May 1933; on Hitler's right can be seen Rudolf Hess, and behind him is vice-Chancellor von Papen, Minister of Labour Franz Seldte, and Transport Minister von Eltz-Ruebenach.* Ph. © Publiphoto

The German Labour Front (*Deutsche Arbeitsfront* or DAF) was the Nazi regime's most important mass organization. It was a substitute for the dissolved trade unions, but it did not have trade union functions, since no freedom of negotiation or association for workers was recognized under the Nazi regime. It was set up on 10 May 1933 as a wing of the National Socialist Party; its head was Robert Ley, one of Hitler's closest collaborators and an official in the top-level NSDAP management. To emphasize the egalitarian character of the organization, the DAF recruited its members among all those involved in production or general working activity, be they employees or employers. This broad-brush approach to recruitment symbolized the total consensus, beyond partisan interests and class

differences, which they wanted to build around the regime. In fact, the DAF was a key factor in Third Reich social policy, since it supported the regime by encouraging the

Above: banners for a "harvest feast" in Hamelin in 1937.
Ph. © Publiphoto
Below: Hitler speaking with Ley (seated), Hess and Frick.

acceptance of collective discipline (not only in the workplace) which constituted one of the cornerstones of Nazi rule. It exerted its greatest influence by having a monopoly over the organization of workers' free time, positioning itself as the instrument of consensus formation and an authentic mouthpiece for the regime's policies. The DAF concerned itself not just with social affairs in the narrow sense, but also with rearmament policy, compelling the acceptance of hardship by the continuous pressure of propaganda; it was especially active in promoting the policy of racism and anti-Semitism. At the height of its powers it organized twenty-five million workers, whose political principles, cultural choices and professional interests it sought to control. Just as in peacetime it manufactured approval around the regime's internal and external policies, in war it sustained the military effort by total political and social mobilization, and mass campaigns increasingly directed at encouraging support from below for Nazi policies of aggression and expansion. All these activities were far removed from the social tone of the DAF's early demagogic phase. ■

(strength through joy) movement, as the system of after-work activities was called.

The regime itself took on the task of removing even the artificial equality between workers and employers which was supposed to derive from their mutual affiliation to the Labour Front. A law on the organization of national work, passed on 20 January 1934, restored the distance between labour and capital by establishing a strongly hierarchical system, formalizing the duty of workers to obey the head of the firm. Even from a semantic point of view this law was extremely significant, as it established unambiguously the relationship of subordination which was to exist between the followers (employees and workers) and the leader (the Führer) — one of the many applications of the *Führerprinzip* on which National Socialist society was founded.

However, what was also obvious in the new organization was the exclusion of workers' representatives, who were not involved in any way in the development of labour relations. The official labour representatives provided for by the law were intended to assist the head of the company in an advisory role rather than as true workers' representatives — they were in effect state representatives within the industrial community. They had to ensure the loyalty of workers to the "national state". On a wider administrative and economic level the official labour representatives were in fact officers of the Reich, whose task consisted essentially of getting the economic policy desired by the Nazi regime applied in practice.

This formal organization of workers, in essence, implemented

The regime's propaganda was centred on the artificial equality between workers and employers, soon belied by reality, and on a strong sense of belonging to the "national state"; the after-work organization and the many popular celebrations and events orchestrated by the Minister for Propaganda, Josef Goebbels, contributed to this. Below: the German Labour Front headquarters, inaugurated by Goebbels during a big festival in Berlin.
Ph. © Publiphoto

Above: Hitler saluted by workers
at a Siemens factory in Berlin,
10 November 1933.
Ph. © Publiphoto
Below: Hitler greeted by a group
of workers engaged in building
the great stadium for Nazi
gatherings in Nuremberg.

the regime's wages policy — which, while breaking the unity and solidarity of trades as well as classes, was aimed at increasing individual productivity, thus creating a situation hardly consistent with collective action. The widespread practice of piecework fell within this rationale: leaving the worker to his own resources ensured his dependence on the regime, without recourse to any trade union organization.

Of course, it was not only propaganda nor merely demagogy that tied workers to the regime. The gradual reduction in unemployment — the problem which finally caused the Weimar Republic to fall apart — provided a most reliable reason for mass approval of the Nazi regime. This was despite the fact that behind the disappearance of unemployment was hidden a tragic deception, in the form of rearmament and preparations for war.

Self-sufficiency and Rearmament

A question that frequently arises is whether the success in the fight against unemployment, which so favoured the Nazi government, could have been achieved under the Weimar Republic, thus preserving democracy? The answer to this cannot be other than negative, especially if one considers that it was, above all, rearmament which contributed to the reduction in unemployment. A second aspect of this was the race against time, which the Weimar Republic lost. Of course, if it could have survived for a few more months and benefited from favourable developments in the international system, the Republic would have overcome its most difficult phase and could gradually have recovered. But this underestimates the role of confidence in the political system as a prerequisite for recovery, and the Republic never possessed such confidence, regardless of whether or not it actually deserved it.

The Minister of Agriculture, Water Darré, speaking at an agriculture festival on the occasion of "Green Week": he is overwhelmed by a gigantic image of Hitler behind him. The symbolism is clear: the Führer holds all the power in his hands. Ph. © Publiphoto

Finally, one last factor worked in favour of the Nazis, although it could equally have worked in favour of the Republic if its political system had in practice shown the resilience that it palpably lacked. What helped the Nazi government was the concentration of power it managed to achieve, which gave it the ability to operate with sufficient speed on several levels. From this perspective the powers in Article 48 of the Weimar constitution would have offered the Republic the legal means to act as a check against the Nazis, but this type of intervention had to be backed up by a solid political base and a clear programme. The Republic lacked all these because of the incompetence of its politicians.

Nazism in power succeeded where the Republic had failed, but at the cost of introducing a factor to which the Republic would never have resorted. What restored the economy to health and resurrected prospects for employment was public

The Krupps, a historic industrial family from Essen involved from the beginning of the nineteenth century in the production of steel and derivatives, supported the Nazi regime, as did many others. Alfred Felix Krupp, who took over the powerful firm in 1943, was later sentenced by an international tribunal to twelve years' imprisonment and then given amnesty in 1951. In the photo, Hitler visits the Krupp steel factories in Essen.
Ph. © Publiphoto
Below: a woman works in a munitions factory. The war necessitated the use of female labour in the arms industry.

spending, in which military spending played a key role, after 1936 becoming the largest source of investment.

Government spending did not simply take the form of generic public works, but rather of contracts mainly aimed at rearmament. This reduced unemployment (which in 1933 still amounted to just under five million people, but by 1934 had already fallen to 2.7 million), and also had the effect of consolidating military support for the regime. The armed forces had disagreed with the Weimar Republic's foreign policy over the questions of the Treaty of Versailles and the re-establishment of Germany's military sovereignty. The Republic had pursued a policy of changing Germany's status in this respect, but by negotiation rather than unilateral action. In contrast the Nazis chose to proceed unilaterally, not through revision of the treaty but through its violation, which made it possible to speed up the pace of change but also rendered it more threatening, with an unambiguous programme which left no one in any doubt as to their true intentions. The support of the Reichswehr and of industry, which also favoured rearmament, represented in this period one of the most solid pillars of the Hitler government.

What is more, industry had no fear of sanctions from the regime. Some doubt might have arisen in the past because of the confused anti-capitalism of some sectors of the NSDAP (including the SA circle and the so-called left of National Socialism), and the corporatist tendencies of some right-wing groups close to the Nazi Party. But in the end an alliance with traditional economic powers proved more advantageous for the Nazis.

A reorganization of relations between the state and industry thus took place, but without jeopardizing the freedom of companies nor their autonomy. The corporatist terminology which was used in political journalism as well as in legislation was not reflected in the creation of any organization which subordinated private power to the power of the state. The industrialists substantially preserved their autonomy; the state limited itself to organizing them into clustered sectors of specialization, managing their links with the administration, reducing raw material quotas and managing currencies. The reorganized relations between the state and the economy never went beyond these limits, not even with the law of 27 February 1934 which provided for an "organic" economic structure.

The creation of the Reich Economic Chamber, which led to the emergence of six large sectors (industry, commerce, banking, insurance, energy, and trades) also reproduced in occupied territories,

By 1935 German aircraft production had reached 300 units per month. Many airplanes would soon be tested during the Spanish Civil War. The photo shows the Messerschmitt logo.

Left: Opel workers take part in a celebration of the company's seventy-fifth anniversary in Russelheim in 1937.
Ph. © Publiphoto

Car production also received a big impetus with the rise of Nazism. In the photo, Hitler greets Auto-Union drivers during a car show at a Berlin festival.
Ph. © Publiphoto

was no more than an acknowledgement of the principle of a hierarchical order. The state's influence operated most strongly through the outlining of objectives, for the attainment of which it required the collaboration and support of economic organizations. In particular there was the need to support heavy industry to facilitate rearmament, and to maintain self-sufficiency in the chemical sector (especially as far as petrol and synthetic rubber were concerned); these examples of the convergence between state interests and industry inter-

ests emphasize the privileged conditions enjoyed by large enterprises under the Third Reich. It was not by accident that the creation of cartels and monopolies, which had already taken off during the Weimar period, speeded up still further, at the expense of the entrepreneurial middle class — who had previously been singled out by NSDAP propaganda as the model of a new economy and the main area which the new regime wished to favour.

The road to rearmament first of all required a secure supply of raw materials for Germany, as well as the guaranteed availability of food in case of a war which would once again isolate Germany from commercial relationships outside of Europe and from the rest of industrialized Europe. The search for self-sufficiency also implied the availability of currency resources to purchase raw materials and food stocks. Here, the collaboration of an economic expert such as Hjalmar Schacht, who as Reichsbank president had strongly opposed the

The Minister of the Economy, Hjalmar Schacht, was a skilled politico-economic strategist: he secured the necessary raw materials for the Reich, which would be increasingly important with the approach of the war, through a policy of subjugation of Balkan countries such as Yugoslavia, Bulgaria and Romania.

Weimar Republic, positioning himself in the ranks of the "national opposition", was essential. Reich Minister of the Economy from 1934, Schacht developed a new politico-economic strategy with the so-called New Plan, which opened Germany to the Balkans and south-east Europe, which was already under Anglo-French influence and heavily affected by the great crisis.

Germany exploited these countries' need for a market for their agricultural and mineral products. It established a new method of commercial payment, moving from a basically multilateral system to bilateral clearing agreements — which, in so far as they did not require currency, helped obviate the need for currency reserves. In this way Germany guaranteed for herself the availability of essential raw materials, and also established a relationship of dependency on the Reich economy by other countries. These were countries at very unequal levels of development and with essentially fragile economic structures, such as Yugoslavia, Romania and Bulgaria. Thus Germany was able to practice currency manipulation and sustain an imbalance between imports and exports.

Successful on the economic and technical level, Schacht's strategy succeeded in political terms as well, as the first step towards securing for the Third Reich a lasting hegemony over all of southern and south-eastern Europe. As a result this area became not just a zone of general German influence, but a veritable German satellite, as finally typified by a March 1939 agreement with Romania which in effect gave Germany a monopoly over oil supplies. Thus, on the eve of the Second World War, Germany secured the supply of fuel necessary to wage a war, and established a model of exploitative relationships that would be applied widely within the framework of the "New European Order".

"History will not judge us for having removed the greatest possible number of men from the economy, but for having created jobs."

Adolf Hitler

The Four-Year Plan

On 9 September 1936, at the NSDAP Nuremberg rally, Hitler launched an economic programme known as the Four-Year Plan. The aims of the plan are known today from a secret memorandum written in August 1935, in which Hitler established that by the end of 1940 the German economy had to be able to withstand a war and the Wehrmacht was to be prepared to wage hostilities.

The plan represented a somewhat new approach by the regime towards political economy, in the sense that if previously the economic recovery had revolved around rearmament and self-sufficiency, now preparation for a war economy became the sole and total objective. The pursuit of self-sufficiency also became an absolute imperative, since complete autonomy in production and in the supply of raw materials needed to be established. In this context it was plain that these developments implied a more rigid control by the state over the economy, and probably more widespread bureaucracy in public life as well as in the economic system. It was a clear political choice by the regime to direct its total energies towards economic and social militarization.

Officially, the Nazi regime's planned objective consisted of securing the internal availability of sufficient essential resources to avoid constraints on demographic growth, an integral part of the Third Reich racial policy: self-sufficiency as a complement to racism. In reality the objective was to speed up rearmament, which necessitated further internal turns of the screw, in turn involving the necessity for collective cohesion and an emphasis on a "social peace" which transcended all real-life conflicts. It was as if Nazism, merely by an act of will, could eradicate the differences and plurality of opposing interests in society. In Hitler's view, in his September 1936 speech, "Faced with the supreme interests of the nation, there are neither employers nor employees but only those operating on behalf of the whole of the people." This was just a glorified vision, words denying the existence of divisions and hierarchies which had in fact been clearly established.

In his secret memorandum, Hitler had specified the final objective which was to be achieved through the efforts imposed on the country: to turn the Wehrmacht into the world's strongest armed force in defence of Germany's demographic devel-

Below: members of the Labour Front march in Hitler's presence at the Nuremberg stadium in November 1937; for the staging of this parade they were expected to hold shovels instead of guns.
Ph. © Publiphoto
Opposite: Propaganda poster for Germany's industrial development.

E/NSATZ
DER DEUTSCHEN KRIEGSMARINE

Rearmament allowed the German navy to build modern battleships and, above all, to reinvigorate its submarine fleet, which had been banned by the Versailles Treaty. Above: propaganda poster for the German navy.
Below: publicity poster for the Reichswerke Hermann Goering, which supported the war industry's big companies.

REICHSWERKE AKTIENGESELLSCHAFT
FÜR WAFFEN- UND MASCHINENBAU „HERMANN GÖRING"
BERLIN W.8 MOHRENSTRASSE 17-19

opment, which ultimately could be guaranteed only by "widening living space [*Lebensraum*] and by the provision of raw material and foodstuffs" for the German people. The future direction of territorial expansion was thus clearly mapped out: the manoeuvres of German foreign policy could be interpreted as a slow march towards these objectives. War was not necessarily preordained, but Germany set about fulfilling its ambitions even at the cost of war: thus could be synthesized the political philosophy implicit in the Four-Year Plan.

The realization of this project involved an organizational structure which necessitated a redistribution of power within the political and administrative apparatus. The disappearance of Schacht from the political scene was one of the consequences of this reorganization. It is unlikely that Schacht left the Ministry of Economics because he was opposed to rearmament, as he would write later. His opposition towards the regime matured later, probably over the management of the economy (the excess of bureaucracy and state control) rather than over its objectives. Certainly, Schacht could have hardly tolerated sharing the management of the economy with a man entirely of party origin such as Hermann Goering. It was to Goering that Hitler assigned the leadership and execution of the Four-Year Plan, underlying the further union between state and party which was one of the key objectives.

In particular the result was an enhanced personal as well as institutional role for Goering, because the powers he enjoyed gave him the opportunity to create a mighty economic conglomerate under his sole direction, the Reichswerke H. Goering. This operated in the mineral and synthetic sectors, and grew fat on the "Aryanization" of Jewish wealth and the plundering of the occupied territories, of which Goering became one of the most ruthless looters in his role as the head of the war economy.

An internal reorganization of the Four-Year Plan's executive in 1938 did not eliminate the confusion of conflicts between management; indeed, it left ample scope for influence on the part of large private companies — in particular the IG Farben chemical monopoly. This increased the blurring of roles between private and public sectors, and especially the collusion between Nazi Party members and industrial leaders, typified in Goering's personal empire.

Apart from all these aspects — which were essential in defining relations between industrial groups and the Nazi regime — it is interesting to note the results of this approach to the management of the German economy. It led to a general

Hitler speaks to the workers at an arms production plant in Berlin in December 1940.
Ph. © Publiphoto

increase in industrial investment, but at the same time a redirection of national output away from consumer goods and towards industrial products. This was a very significant trend which can be expressed in other terms: during the war less consumer goods were produced than in 1938, while basic production increased (especially in the chemical sector) and arms production more than quadrupled in comparison with the period immediately before the war, until it reached a peak in 1944, at the height of the war effort.

Chapter 6

WAR AND THE **N**EW **E**UROPEAN **O**RDER

THE ANNEXATION OF AUSTRIA. THE INVASION OF CZECHOSLOVAKIA. THE ATTACK ON POLAND. BETWEEN 1938 AND 1939 GERMANY SET ABOUT ESTABLISHING THE "NEW EUROPEAN ORDER". FACILITATED BY APPEASEMENT BY WESTERN DEMOCRACIES, THIS LED TO NAZI DOMINATION OF CONTINENTAL EUROPE BY 1942.

Between 1938 and 1939, by annexing Austria and overrunning Czechoslovakia, the first phase of the National Socialist programme of establishing German supremacy in Europe (and possibly the world) had been accomplished. The creation of the Great German Reich was the first fulfilment of Germany's territorial claims. This consisted of the absorption within the Reich of German national communities outside its borders, for example in Austria and German Sudetenland, in accordance with the programme outlined in *Mein Kampf* and with the imperatives of German foreign policy. However, later events showed that the reunification of German-speaking peoples into the Great Reich was not an end in itself: behind the assertion of nationality lay more important and longer-term objectives.

Even before the rise of Nazism, Hitler recognized Fascism's legacy in the battle against Bolshevism and the dismantlement of institutions by squadrismo *methods. In the photo: Hitler and Mussolini in Florence during the Führer's trip to Italy in May 1938.*
Ph. © Publiphoto

A Programme of Aggression

After the establishment of the Four-Year Plan, Germany's objective of territorial expansion moved into a concrete and operational phase: the conquest of the "vital space", theorized by Hitler since the 1920s, acquired a more defined char-

In August 1936 the last Olympic Games before the war took place in Berlin (the next would not be held until 1948). The event was enormously exploited by the regime's propaganda machine — Hitler used it to celebrate "the strength and beauty of the German people" — and the many prestigious guests enjoyed luxurious surroundings. Anti-Jewish signs in the streets were removed for the occasion. In the photo: foreign competitors enter the Berlin stadium.

The annexation of Austria was approved by a unanimous vote on 10 April 1938.
Below: propaganda for the vote — "The people say yes!"

acter. The re-establishment of German military sovereignty, pursued by the Nazi regime to escape from the strictures of the Versailles Treaty — and in particular the reintroduction of compulsory military service in 1935 and the remilitarization of the Rhineland in the early months of 1936 — was dictated not by prestige, but was one of the prerequisites for launching an active phase of foreign policy. In February 1938 the replacement of the commanders of the diplomatic corps and the Wehrmacht with high-level Nazi apparatchiks (in the Ministry of Foreign Affairs, the conservative von Neurath was replaced by a "diplomat" of National Socialist origin, Joachim von Ribbentrop) marked a new aggressive phase in the Third Reich's policy.

In March 1938 the Austrian *Anschluss* represented the first step outside the boundaries established at Versailles and strengthened Germany's control and influence over South and South-Eastern Europe, which was already heavily dependent on the German economy. The Munich pact of September 1938 was centred around the withdrawal of France and Britain from the political and diplomatic scene in East-Central Europe and this void had great significance for the Third Reich in its strategy of aggression towards the east. The collapse of Czechoslovakia, with the transfer of the Sudetenland to the Reich as agreed at the Munich conference, opened up for Germany the definite possibility of expansion eastwards.

Military, Political and Strategic Alliances

Ever since her intervention in the Spanish Civil War in July 1936, Germany had shown that she wanted to play an active part in European politics, in keeping with her renewed position as a great power, along with Fascist Italy, with which she had obvious common strategic, political, ideologi-

During the Spanish Civil War, Germany and Italy supported the rebellious nationalists. Above: Hitler and Franco at the frontier between France and Spain. Below: the signing of the Munich Pact; from left, Chamberlain, Daladier, Hitler, Mussolini and Ciano. Ph. © Publiphoto

cal and diplomatic interests. From this moment on, the Nazi-Fascist alliance became an important factor in disrupting the equilibrium established in the peace treaties — without it, the crisis in international relations and the slide towards war would not have been possible. The Munich pact was also the result of complicity between Italy and Germany. Italy had been isolated as a consequence of her foray into Ethiopia in 1935–36, and her support was crucial in permitting Germany's painless accomplishment of the Austrian *Anschluss.*

While the policy of appeasement followed by Western democracies assured Germany that the breakdown of the European order established at Versailles could be accomplished in an unhindered fashion, it is not clear exactly when Germany decided on the various phases of her territorial expansion. In a meeting with military leaders on 5 November 1937, Hitler laid down some explicit scenarios which included military intervention to resolve the "German question" not later than 1943–45, or even before if circumstances permitted. The "German question" was the question of German space; the absorption of Austria and Czechoslovakia was nothing but the first step in a new march towards the East in a strategy of continental domination. There is no doubt that during 1939 what had so far been the threatening but vague slogan *Lebensraum* acquired a more precise meaning, with the claim of a "great space" which would be subject to Germany's economic hegemony. This claim had two functions: it established the long-term objective of expansion of the Great Reich; and it established a mechanism which would consolidate the Third Reich's preparation for war, as had already happened in the case of the oil agreement with Romania.

With the Munich Pact the Western powers abdicated control over East-Central Europe: Czechoslovakia was forced to surrender "peacefully" to Germany the Sudetenland, inhabited by three million German-speaking people. In the photo: the front of a house is covered with swastikas and Hitler's portrait, awaiting the arrival of the German troops.
Ph. © Publiphoto

After Munich and the so-called Pact of Steel with Italy (in May 1939), which limited Italy's interests to the Mediterranean and left a free hand to the Reich in the area of the Danube, the path towards German expansion was further defined and strengthened by the economic interest of almost all sectors of German industry in securing sources of raw materials in the East. This in a sense provided further legitimization for more territorial conquest. From this perspective,

The non-aggression pact was signed on 23 August 1939 in Moscow by Foreign Ministers von Ribbentrop and Molotov. The Soviet Union, engaged in a war against Japan in Mongolia, feared another war without allies. In the photo: Stalin and von Ribbentrop after signing the agreement.

the German-Soviet Pact of 23 August 1939 protected Germany against the clear danger of a war on two fronts, given France and Britain's predictable opposition to German military action against Poland. However, the non-aggression pact, which allowed for the partition of Poland, also limited the Third Reich's prospects for expansion. But this was only an illusion, because the very reasons which made the USSR accept a truce with Nazi Germany were the same reasons Germany offered a truce to the USSR, which she was in fact ready to invade as soon as the opportunity arose.

The relationship established between Fascist Italy and Nazi Germany, even before the formal pact of alliance (the Pact of Steel) concluded on 22 May 1939, was not only political and diplomatic. It also had a strongly ideological character, an authentic rapport of affinity and solidarity between regimes. Even before the Nazis' rise to power, Hitler recognized Fascism's importance in the battle against Bolshevism, and also in the dismantlement of democratic parliamentary institutions and labour movement organizations. He saw *squadrismo* and the march on Rome as examples of the new methods of political battle; these tactics were later copied by the National Socialist movement. Italian Fascism was more cautious in recognizing its affinity with National Socialism, for reasons which had to do more with Italy's

interests as a power than with doctrinal differences (though it is true that in the beginning racism, and in particular anti-Semitism, were alien to Fascism). In fact, Italy's "revisionism" coincided only partly with that of Nazi Germany. However, after 1933 the logic of affinity prevailed, despite the potential conflict with Germany over control of the Danube, which was resolved at the expense of the First Austrian Republic.

After her conquest of Ethiopia in 1935, international isolation led Italy to accept an alliance of subordination with Nazi Germany. Consolidated by the two countries' simultaneous intervention in the Spanish Civil War, this alliance continued further, not only in the shape of the Munich Pact of 1938, but also with the explosion of a racist campaign in Italy. This, while not being directly influenced by Germany, represented a further step towards Fascism's

ideological and cultural subordination to Nazi Germany. After intervention in the war and the pitiful failure of the attempt at "parallel war", Italy's role of subjection could not be rescued even by the privileged personal relationship which Hitler maintained with Mussolini. The crisis which the regime experienced in July 1943 finally shook German confidence in Italy and in Fascism. After the armistice on 8 September 1943, the occupation of Italy by the Wehrmacht created the ambivalent situation of having an "occupied ally", as has recently been recognized by the historian Klinkhammer. Only Hitler's interest in keeping Mussolini's persona and image alive, and the imperatives of state which necessitated a public demonstration of the continuance of the alliance for the benefit of international observers, justified the existence of an overtly autonomous social Republic of Italy. In fact the Republic was increasingly tied, through the Nazification of the Fascists of Salò, with the Third Reich, which exploited Italy for its war economy and as a defensive bulwark in the Mediterranean area. ■

Stamp immortalizing the Italian-German alliance. Below: Hitler in Italy in 1938. Opposite, above: strategic meeting between Mussolini and Hitler in Salzburg, 1942; below: a French cartoon showing Hitler extorting Mussolini's support for the war.

France was defeated in only six weeks; Paris surrendered on 14 June 1940 and remained under German rule until 24 August 1944. With the conquest of France, the Third Reich inaugurated the New European Order, assigning to itself the role of the "power of order in Europe". In the photo: Hitler in Paris, 1940.

Ph. © Publiphoto

The Plan for European Domination

The plan to achieve European autonomy from the point of view of raw materials and manufacturing processes (continental self-sufficiency under German leadership) now took the form of resurrecting and re-emphasizing old concepts (such as that of *Mitteleuropa*) which had been developed during the First World War. However, it could not be separated from the more comprehensive plan for specifically Nazi political, social and racial domination, which was taking shape during the subjugation of Europe.

The slogan *Neuordnung Europas,* the New European Order or even world order, was used in propaganda to glorify the Third Reich's plans of conquest during the war. After the defeat of France in June 1940, when it seemed nothing could stop the Wehrmacht and it also looked like the eve of a British capitulation, the Nazi leadership tried to define the New European Order more precisely, going beyond generic imperialistic ambitions towards Europe and the general objective of restoring the German Empire (possibly in Africa).

The most staunch supporters of German ambitions were the Minister for Propaganda, Joseph Goebbels, and the Minister of the Economy, Walther Funk. Goebbels tried to develop a specifically European Nazi ideology. Within these limits, the Reich's essential function was that of a "guarantor of European order", and the "Hitler state [appeared] as the heir and restorer of a great empire".

When, after the collapse of France, the time came for Britain to be isolated, Goebbels played the New Order card to gain the support of continental Europe in favour of the Third Reich, denouncing Britain as the impoverisher of the continent. Later, after the invasion of the Soviet Union in June 1941, the New European ideology acquired a deep anti-Bolshevik tinge, in order to present the Third Reich's European project as the sole bulwark against the Bolshevik peril. In this way it was used to justify both German aggression and Germany's expansionist ambitions. In summary, the Reich was portrayed

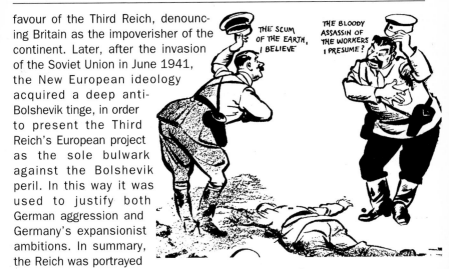

as leading a great coalition of peoples invited to mobilize (but only as collaborators) against the Asiatic Bolshevik threat.

Walther Funk was the most active supporter of the *Grossraumwirtschaft*, which advocated a strategy of continental self-sufficiency under the hegemony of the Third Reich. The economy of this "great space" would be based on more than just the subordination of European production systems to German supremacy, with different treatment accorded to Western and Eastern Europe. Highly-industrialized France would keep a privileged position almost as a partner, albeit a dependent one, of the Reich. On the other hand, the countries of Eastern and South-Eastern Europe, whatever their destiny as states, were to be kept in a permanent state of underdevelopment: in fact, they would not be allowed to undergo any real process of industrialization, as their function was and must remain that of a food and manpower reserve for the Reich.

The "great space" was to mean, above all, the penetration by German industrial and financial power of the production and financial systems of the periphery of Europe. The resources of the latter were to converge towards a dominant centre in

It was clear that the German-Soviet non-aggression pact was a temporary postponement of the Nazi programme to fight Communism; on 22 June 1941, with Operation Redbeard, Hitler invaded Russia. In the picture, an English cartoon satirizes the agreement.

*T*wo French cartoons illustrate the politics of expansion of the Reich. Above: a Polish soldier stops German access to the "corridor" between East Prussia and Germany. Below: Chamberlain and Daladier prevent Hitler from grabbing another "bunch" of territories.

the shape of the Reich, at the top of an ideal pyramid of values. This idea reiterated the theory of the role of a great power, excluding all other powers, developed in the field of international law by Carl Schmitt.

Finally, the concept of the New European Order enshrined racist, geopolitical and militaristic motivations, which represented different components of Nazi imperialism and had developed through a long theoretical and doctrinal process ever since the 1920s (from the prophecies of Moeller van den Bruck and Oswald Spengler to the more recent and refined "Monroe Doctrine for Europe" elaborated by Carl Schmitt). On these principles was based the hierarchy of the states, whereby small states were condemned to virtual non-existence, playing the role of mere onlookers within an even more rigid hierarchy of race and people. It was a theory which lacked any historical or scientific ground and which was justified only by its function in relation to the German role as a dominant power and, in practice, as the arbiter of continental Europe's destiny.

It must not be overlooked that one of the principles on which the attempt to restructure Europe by force was based was the establishment of the idea of the superiority of the German people as *Herrenvolk*. This was a principle designed to legitimize the supremacy of the German people in all fields (to the point where, in some circumstances, only Germans had the right to own land). It was also used to justify anti-Semitism and anti-Slavism, and the hostility towards all ethnic and social groups considered *minderwerting* (inferior), from gypsies to homosexuals and any other so-called "asocial" communities not compatible with the cultural and social parameters considered typical of Germans.

It was this racist intransigence and lack of respect for other nationalities which made the offers of collaboration, put forward in various guises by the Nazis in areas of occupied Europe, only partially successful. They gained most ground in the cultural environments of Western and Northern Europe (from France to Norway), where there were ideological links with the Germans based on previous pro-Fascist and pro-Nazi tendencies. They were naturally rejected where their acceptance would have meant — especially in the Slavic countries — inevitable national and cultural suicide.

The French Vichy government, established in July 1940, adopted a policy of substantial collaboration with the Nazi regime: Marshall Petain told the country that he chose collaboration because he was forced to by the aggressor, but in reality the government took the initiative.
Above: posters in Paris promoting the Nazis' anti-Bolshevik struggle. Below: the four "menaces" to French peace in a 1941 poster: freemasonry, Jews, de Gaulle and mendacity.

Implementing the New European Order

The invasion of Poland on 1 September 1939 opened the path to the completion of the Nazi plan. In Poland the methods essential to the realization of the great project of enforced European integration were applied for the first time, even though at the time of Poland's occupation the boundaries of a Europe dominated by Germany could not yet be foreseen. However, developments in Poland — which had been invaded, divided and had disintegrated, both as a state and a national unit — soon raised the problem of the nature of the objectives the Third Reich intended to pursue in the occupied territories. Far from representing an isolated case, the Polish experience proved to be an example, albeit extreme, in the phenomenon of Nazi domination in Europe. This was because of the severity of every aspect of occupation, to the extent of the physical eradication of the country's inhabitants. The population was destined to have no future and at best (that is, if they were to survive physically) to be a reserve of slave labour for Germany, deprived of any national individuality and totally subject to the labour market demands of the Third Reich.

Poland showed that the policy of extermination operated by the German forces, not only the special SS units but also the Wehrmacht, was not an accident resulting from the imperatives of defence or linked to war operations. It was a predetermined policy, part of the conception of war as a preventative instrument in the battle between mutually-exclusive peoples and races. The management of the war by the Nazis meant that the brutality of extermination was, because of the way it was organized, an ingrained objective of the Third Reich: domination in Europe was not possible without genocide. For this reason the Nazi war was, and had to be, a war of extermination.

The invasion of Poland was one of the first practical demonstrations of a new way of fighting called Blitzkrieg *— lightning war. After the occupation the three million Jews in the country were herded into ghettos and used as forced labour. Above: German soldiers break a barrier on the frontier between Germany and Poland in the first hours of the invasion.*
Ph. © Publiphoto
Below: Jews in the Warsaw ghetto are put on a lorry for transfer to labour camps.

The occupation of a large part of Europe, especially in the east, was not aimed solely at the exercise of command and control power in a determined area for military ends; it was also a means of "Germanizing" the territories east of the Reich. This could only be achieved by pushing the population further eastwards, or simply eliminating them. This attitude could not be regarded as defensive, nor was it due to any imminent aggression against Germany or sudden uprising against the German occupying forces. It was simply due to the need to assert the right of the Germans — the right of the strongest — to be in sole control of who would live and who would die, of which countries would enjoy economic development and which would not, using intimidation as an instrument to "normalize" situations which could by no stretch of the imagination be described as peaceful or normal.

The Germanization of Europe

The Polish model was applied to the occupied territories of Yugoslavia and the Soviet Union. The Second World War was a total (or totalitarian) war because of the indiscriminate way Germany involved whole populations, nations and ethnic communities in pursuit of a precise and partisan ideological position. She did this in the interests of power and racial exclusivity; it was irrelevant whether or not any hostility was exercised towards her or her soldiers. To understand that the destruction of whole national groups and state systems was essential to the Germanization of Europe — which could be realized only in this way — one must understand the rationality of a process which would otherwise seem incomprehensible.

The mass of ruins to which Poland and the occupied territories of Soviet Union and Yugoslavia were reduced was not the result of blind savagery, but the outcome of a preordained and planned project. "Night and Fog", code-name of a notorious Nazi order for the deportation of partisans and hostages, was unwittingly destined to serve as a metaphor for the situation in Europe under Nazi domination.

The Europe to be Germanized reached its maximum territorial dimensions at the end of 1942, before the military reversals which set in after the capitulation of the German army at Stalingrad. Beginning from the west, Greater Germany extended towards the east and south-east with the annexation of Poland (Danzig, West Prussia province and Warthegau), Belgium (Euoen and Malmedy), France (Alsace-Lorraine), Luxembourg and Slovenia. It was at the centre of a complex system of territories and states with very diverse legal frameworks, which can be classified as follows.

• Territories under Germany's direct domination (the government-general of a subjugated Poland; the Protectorate of Bohemia and Moravia; occu-

London, 3 September 1939: a newspaper placard announces the declaration of war.

Til vakt ved Nordens grense mot øst
ᛋᛋ-SKIJEGERBATALJON
NORGE

Norway represented a territory of great strategic importance, both for its mineral resources and for its position, which permitted the control of the entire coastline east of Greenland. The Norwegian army surrendered to the Germans on June 1940; some troops later joined the Nazis against the Red Army. In the picture, a Norwegian propaganda poster encourages recruitment to the Waffen-SS.

pied Belgium; Yugoslavia, split between Italy and Germany following the annexation of Slovenia, and totally fragmented after the dismemberment of the rest of the country between Germany, Italy, Hungary and Bulgaria; the satellite state of Croatia and Serbia, created in a state of semi-colonial dependency towards the Reich; Greece; and the occupied Soviet territories).

● Denmark, Norway, Holland and Vichy France (from November 1942 also subject to direct military occupation), where some residual appearance of sovereignty did not conceal their real condition of servitude and subjection towards Germany.

● The allies of the Tripartite Pact (most importantly Italy, which after the armistice of 8 September 1943 had to suffer German occupation as well), Finland, Rumania, Hungary (occupied in March 1944), Bulgaria and Czechoslovakia, all satellites under the political and military hegemony of the Great Reich.

A substantial proportion of these territories — certainly Poland and the occupied Soviet territories — were condemned to permanent indiscriminate exploitation and deprivation of national identity, functioning only in the interests of the Reich and the physical expansion of the German population. Bastions of German defence between Europe and Asia, they were territories destined for direct Germanization through the transfer of populations from the old Reich, as well as for indirect Germanization through the deportation of tens of millions of previous inhabitants (an operation which included the physical decimation of these same populations) or through the re-Germanization of limited groups of the population considered suitable for assimilation within the German people. In these territories the principle of the racial supremacy of the German people was applied most enthusiastically.

In the midst of war uncertainty hung over the

destiny of substantial parts of the occupied areas, split between German military and civil administrations, and often run by puppet governments of collaborators. These were not only the result of the imposition of occupying power, but also a sign of the deep-rooted Fascism and Nazism which existed in Europe. The national divisions left by the First World War allowed minority groups of nationalists to assign to Nazi Germany the task of re-establishing national rights which had not been recognized by the peace treaties. Seldom could hopes have been more completely frustrated, for the Nazi regime was opposed by definition to every principle of equality between nations.

In 1942 the Axis countries had achieved their maximum territorial expansion. Prisoners from the occupied territories, mainly Jews, were deported to concentration camps spread all over Europe, particularly in Germany and Eastern Europe. From the moment the "final solution" to the Jewish question was decided, concentration camps increasingly became places of death, in accordance with the politics of mass genocide.

OCCUPIED TERRITORIES AND EXTERMINATION CAMPS IN 1942

- Axis countries
- Axis satellites
- Militarily-occupied countries
- Allies
- Neutral countries
- △ Labour camps
- ▲ **Extermination camps**

Chapter 7

CONCENTRATION
CAMPS AND
GENOCIDE

THE CONCENTRATION AND EXTERMINATION CAMPS WERE THE INSTRUMENT BY WHICH NAZISM IMPLEMENTED ITS COLONIZATION PLANS AND AFFIRMED THE POWER OF THE GERMAN RACE, THROUGH THE DESTRUCTION OF WHOLE POPULATIONS AND OF MILLIONS OF JEWS IN THE OCCUPIED TERRITORIES.

We have already alluded to the importance of the concentration camps in the first phase of Nazism's establishment in power, and their use in the repression of the Third Reich's enemies — starting with what from March 1933 became the archetypal model for such camps, the *lager* at Dachau, near Munich. However, it is important to stress that while these camps had a temporary character in the first two years of power, they became in subsequent years a permanent institution which was continuously developed and further expanded by the war.

The Concentration Camp System

It is important to remind ourselves that the concentration camps were not a matter of degeneration in, but a direct expression of, the Nazi system: they were integral, and not additional, to the system; not a development which was an end in itself, but a phenomenon designed to affect deeply the process of disciplining the German people. Later, after the war began and Nazi domination extended throughout Europe, the most destructive element prevailed: the denial of the

Children behind the barbed wire of a Nazi concentration camp in Carelia (in the USSR, near Finland) in the summer of 1944. During the war the system of concentration camps created by the Nazis — initially to eliminate political enemies and all those who for one reason or another were considered undesirable by the regime — turned into a ruthless and efficient machine for mass extermination. The sign in the picture reads "clearing camp", innocently enough, but the following text gives an idea of how different things were in reality: "Entry into the camp and conversation through the fence are punishable by shooting".
Ph. © Publiphoto

A road sign in Mauthausen, the Austrian site of one of the most important extermination camps. In six years more than 35,000 people were killed there. Below: the camp entrance, today transformed into a "sanctuary" open to the public.

right to live to people considered unworthy of life, as part of the exacerbation of the political and racial battle.

The main feature of the system was its institutionalization, which made it an autonomous instrument of the SS and the police, especially after the fusion in 1936 of the supreme offices of the two bodies in the person of Himmler. People were not sent to concentration camps to serve a sentence of imprisonment set by the judicial authorities, but in general only to avoid them causing political inconvenience. The political police could decide arbitrarily to get rid of anybody who was suspected of being out of line with the regime, without the person necessarily being an active opponent of Nazism. The rules defining Himmler's powers and the characteristics of the so-called *Schutzhaft* (preventive detention) progressively removed every limitation to the powers of the police.

In 1938, with the extension of deportation to the concentration camps to the "asocial", the powers of the Gestapo were increased and forced labour was introduced in the camps, together with SS economic enterprises which used the prisoners' manpower. The year 1938 was also significant for the concentration camp system for other reasons: first of all, the Austrian *Anschluss* extended both the Gestapo's area of authority and the camp network itself. To Dachau, Sachsenhausen, Buchenwald and Flossenburg was now added Mauthausen, near Linz. Secondly, after the November pogrom (the Night of Broken Glass) some tens of thousands of Jews were transferred to the camps, thus anticipating in a sinister manner the role of the concentration camps in the solution to the Jewish question. In May 1939, the *lager* map was enlarged with the creation of a camp specifically for women at Ravensbruck.

The outbreak of war increased the proliferation and role of the concentration camps. In the preceding five years the direction of the camps had acquired a specific autonomy within the Nazi power system. From an institutional point of view, they were the most concrete examples of the overthrow of the old judiciary; special groups of men, the Death's Head units, were developed within the SS to supervise the camps.

Above: an officer of the special SS Death's Head unit for camp surveillance supervises Mauthausen prisoners going to carry out forced labour.

The camps became a school for violence, not only for the prisoners but also for the troops in charge of their supervision, who were asked to be inflexible and extremely detached with the prisoners, viewing them as objects rather than persons. The camp at Dachau became the model of SS organization, but also a model for the treatment of prisoners: they were subject to rigid and often absurd rules of discipline, harsh psychological conditions, arbitrary ill treatment and corporal punishment. It was an authentic regime of terror, only superficially masked at first as having re-educational objectives. Prisoners did not have any sentence to serve — their only crime was their existence.

Left: an SS officer, member of the Gestapo's political branch, takes a roll-call of prisoners destined for the gallows.
Ph. © Publiphoto

The concentration camp in Auschwitz (the German name for the Polish town of Oshwieçim, fifty kilometres west of Cracow), showing the barbed wire enclosure and the long line of barracks where the prisoners lived.

Ph. © Publiphoto

There was a rigid hierarchy inside the camps; after 1936 common criminals were sent there, and were often entrusted with the task of running the camps. This confusion between torturers and victims made coexistence and the survival of prisoners even more difficult; the mechanisms of community segregation were pushed to their limits.

The introduction of distinctive symbols for every category of prisoner (a red triangle for political prisoners, pink for homosexuals, green for ordinary criminals, black for the "anti-social", lilac for Jehovah's Witnesses, and yellow for Jews, normally with the addition of another colour) corresponded to a logic of classification but also emphasized the distinction between the prisoners themselves, so they lacked any homogeneity.

It has been pointed out that the war marked a break in the development of the concentration camp system. On the one hand it was extended to occupied or annexed territories (as early as 1940 the Natzweiler camp in Alsace and Auschwitz in ex-Polish territory were opened); on the other hand the war resulted in changes in the functions of the camps. Prisoner-of-war camps

were added to most *lager*, especially after the invasion of the USSR. The population of the camps, which until 1939 had been composed mainly of Germans, was radically changed by the arrival of prisoners from all over occupied Europe, leaving Germans as a small minority. The population of the camps also grew because of the increased rigour of persecutions and raids resulting from security fears and the paranoia associated with war. Moreover, the greater frequency with which death sentences were passed often turned the camps into places of execution, and this further increased their function of intimidation.

During 1942 the role of the camps underwent another change: in March they were given over to the SS economic administration. Because of the difficulty in obtaining sufficient manpower for war industries, the SS experimented with using prisoners as forced labour — which often amounted to another technique for their physical elimination. In

general this kind of forced labour was used in aircraft construction and (especially in the underground factories of Buchenwald) the development of missiles designed to bombard England. The prime example of this use of forced labour was Auschwitz, which was planned to be the largest concentration camp complex, containing in Birkenau no fewer than 100,000 deported people to be used in industrial plants (like those of IG Farben) built in the surrounding area.

During the war, concentration camps became extermination camps equipped with gas chambers and crematoria that were used with great ruthlessness for the physical elimination of Jews. In these camps the annihilation of human lives

Top: men from British ships sunk in the Atlantic by the Germans are taken to a concentration camp.
Bottom: prisoners doing forced labour in the Zajezierze camp in Poland.
Ph. © Publiphoto

"Scientific" experiments with human guinea-pigs in the Dachau camp. Right: a prisoner dressed in overalls is submerged for hours in a bath filled with iced water to test his resistance to freezing conditions. Doctors Holzloehner (left) and Rascher (right) are conducting the experiment. Below: the suffering of a Jewish prisoner regaining consciousness after being placed in a pressure chamber.
Ph. © Publiphoto

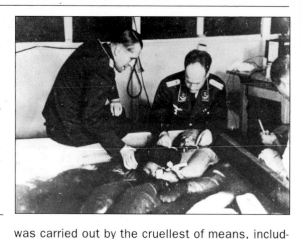

was carried out by the cruellest of means, including the most degrading and exhausting work, and medical experiments carried out on behalf of the SS by ruthless doctors and pseudo-scientists acting merely out of sadism, with no conceivable scientific objectives.

There are no reliable statistics on the millions of people who went through concentration and extermination camps: they probably numbered around twenty million. There is no precise evidence of the number of Germans involved in the creation and direction of the camps, from their supervision to the organization of transport services; they may number many hundreds of thousands of people — perhaps one million. These figures indicate the dimension of the tragedy experienced by such a large proportion of the population of Europe, and also of the collective experience undergone by German society, resulting in a heritage of culpability, attitudes and behaviours which are difficult to understand and totally unacceptable in a civilized world.

Movement and Decimation of Populations

The violence used in the segregation, concentration

and extermination camps was not circumscribed. In a sense, it became the way of life of a society. After all, even before being transferred outside the Reich's boundaries, the practice of murder for biogenic ends had already been largely adopted in a law of July 1933 which had legalized compulsory sterilization for those suffering from hereditary illness, physical handicap and mental illness.

By the same token, at the end of 1939 the practice of compulsory euthanasia was authorized, resulting in the murder of inmates in psychiatric institutions between 1940 and 1941. In that year the regime was obliged to suspend this operation following protests, notably from Church representatives. It is estimated that 120,000 patients were killed in this foretaste and general test of the mass killing planned for the elimination of Jews.

A similar lack of consideration for the value of human life characterized the whole range of methods used by the Third Reich's executive bodies to assert domination in occupied territories. This was true in the case of Poland, which was used as an experiment in view of plans to eliminate other Slavic populations after the invasion of the Soviet Union, and for the physical liq-

*A*bove: a crematorium at the Buchenwald camp in Germany. As extermination operations intensified, camp administrators commissioned increasingly powerful crematoria, designed and manufactured by German firms.
Ph. © Publiphoto
Below left: the terrible steep stairway with 180 steps which Mauthausen prisoners had to climb to gain access to a stone quarry.
Ph. © Publiphoto
Below right: forced labourers loaded with stones ascend the stairway.

The chilling scene found by an American journalist who arrived at the Buchenwald camp with the Allied troops: the ground was covered with hundreds of corpses which the Germans had not had time to burn or bury.
Ph. © Publiphoto

uidation of the Jewish population.

Their crude biological warfare was based on the one hand on the assumption of the lower value of inferior peoples, and on the other on the assertion of German superiority — racial, certainly, but also in terms of military strength. This explains the ferocity of the battle, and also the transformation in educational values and in the behaviour of individual German citizens in uniform (and even those not in uniform). They were conditioned to exalt their own race, even before national superiority, and were therefore guaranteed immunity in committing any acts of violence which could be justified in the name of the Great Reich's fortunes.

In Poland the elimination of state identity was only the first step. Next came the eradication of national culture through the closure of schools, the abolition of university education and the limitation of literacy — all measures which were a complete reversal of historical development but conformed with the practice of genocide. The essential features of national identity were destroyed through barbarism, by reducing the population of a now nameless territory to a state of enslavement under the Germans; at the same time the élite representatives of national culture and the Jewish population were murdered, at first gradually and then with speeded-up mass methods.

Similar practices were used in the Soviet Union. Even before the invasion of the USSR the Wehrmacht supreme command issued, on 6 June 1941, the so-called *Kommissarbefehl*, which provided for the killing of Red Army political commissioners taken prisoner by the Germans. Ideological and racial hatred were enshrined in provisions which effectively guaranteed immunity for anybody making an attempt on the lives of Soviet citizens.

Soviet soldiers surrender to the Germans. Soviet prisoners falling into Nazi hands during the Russian campaign were put in concentration and labour camps. They died in thousands, decimated by exhaustion, illness, hunger and cold.

The systematic elimination of Soviet prisoners of war was a deliberate strategy in a policy of mass murder designed to hit not only the managerial élite of the Soviet state, but also to inflict a fatal blow on the demographic strength of the USSR. The deportation for forced labour of Soviet citizens — who were mercilessly exposed to hunger, illness and reprisals — was merely another way of eliminating undesirable human beings who were considered inferior.

In East-Central Europe, Germany applied a relentless policy of racial exploitation and intolerance which was not replicated in occupied Western Europe, because it was in the east that Germanization was to be applied without compromise. Western Europe saw nothing comparable to the so-called *Generalplan Ost*, developed between 1941 and 1942, and certainly the most ambitious expression of German expansionist goals towards the east.

Combined with the plans for the "final solution", about which more will be said, the

A monitor commemorates the victims of the Flossenburg camp in Germany, divided by nationality. At the top are the Russians (26,430 victims) and the Polish (17,546 victims). The total number of people killed was 73,296. Below: the Flossenburg camp.
Ph. © Publiphoto

Generalplan Ost — nowadays known only in its broad outlines — was designed to modify physically the relationships between populations in occupied Eastern Europe. Without entering into details, it is sufficient to say that the plan reflected the European dimension of the Nazi programme, both in its objectives and in the means chosen to implement it. In a historical perspective, it showed the continuity of Nazi ambitions with the traditional ideas of German imperialism.

It was a massive plan of territorial conquest in the east (which presupposed, after the elimination of Poland, the destruction of the USSR as a state), involving a huge transformation in the panorama of diverse nationalities in the light of the central idea of Germanization.

The plan's objective was to guarantee Germany's future security in the east through wide territorial conquest, followed by a huge operation of colonization within the new boundaries. The affirmation of German racial supremacy through the biological repression and destruction of the other peoples in the area would be the instrument with which territorial conquest was transformed into a permanent reality.

As complete and synchronized Germanization of the occupied area was obviously not possible, it was thought best to start with the transplantation of German populations into those territories destined to form the final boundaries of this empire: a sort of security zone as an immediate bulwark against the Asian bloc.

The whole project would take a

considerable period of time to realize — about thirty years. Tens of millions of people, taking natural demographic movements into account, would be involved in a process which encompassed the physical elimination of Jews and other minorities, forced transfers of Slavic populations, their substitution with Germanic groups, and the rehabilitation of "Germanizable" elements. This redefinition of the map of populations would imply a revision of social hierarchies; in fact, the settlements of Germanic groups would be essentially urban, linked to the ownership of urban land (reserved for Germans) and the development of industrial activities in which the interests of the various sectors of German production converged.

Lines of graves with the names of more than 33,000 victims of Nazi extermination in the national cemetery of Terezin (a town near Prague in Czechoslovakia, at the time called Theresienstadt and the site of a Jewish ghetto).
Ph. © Publiphoto

In the past, German minorities living in Central, Eastern and South-Eastern Europe had been used as a means of destabilizing the governments of states heavily troubled by national rivalries (particularly in Czechoslovakia and Yugoslavia), to the point that the Dutch historian De Jong openly spoke of their function as a "fifth column". In the same way, the groups of German colonists were now to represent the racial élite and, at the same time, hold the positions of greatest political and social power.

The project was never completely defined in terms of its final goals, nor could it be taken to its ultimate conclusion, as the war proved a serious obstacle to its realization. However, its first steps were sufficient to confirm the system of discrimination and privileges benefiting the Great Reich which would constitute the foundations of the Europe of the New Order. In the long run the colonization would prove to be at the expense of

Below: prisoners in the Jewish ghetto in Lodz, Poland, with the yellow Star of David on their clothes.
Opposite: scenes from the ghettos in Lodz (top) and Warsaw (middle and bottom).

the German peoples whom the Third Reich transferred by force into the occupied eastern territories: in 1944–45 they were pushed back by force towards the German frontiers, soon afterwards to be moved further westwards.

The "Final Solution" and the Genocide of Jews

It has already been stated that with the outbreak of the war even the persecution of Jews acquired a new character, if for no other reason than because the possibility of emigration vanished; what is more, Germany's expansion involved an extension of its domination over millions of Jews spread throughout the continent, particularly in the east.

With hindsight, the threats of destruction of the "Jewish race" repeatedly uttered by Hitler and other Nazi leaders before the outbreak of war can by no stretch of the imagination be regarded

merely as propaganda. It is not known when exactly the expression "final solution" was formulated; it was certainly first used in March 1941. However, from mid-September 1939 massive transfers of Jews had been organized by the Germans in the zones of occupied Poland, in order to concentrate them in prescribed urban areas. It was the first step towards the creation of large ghettos, which were still considered to be a "temporary solution" to the Jewish question.

These measures already used a great deal of violence, but their implementation by Himmler, now also commissioner for the consolidation of the German race, amounted to a continuous chain of deportations, slaughters and gratuitous brutality. In Lodz, the industrial textiles city renamed Litzmannstadt, Jews were excluded from the distribution of foodstuffs even before they were relegated to the ghettos. The first mass expulsion was ordered by Himmler on 30 October 1939 as part of the deportation of Polish people, in particular Jews, from the territories of ex-Poland now annexed to the Reich. After the invasion of Western Europe by the

Wehrmacht, the Jews of France, Belgium and Holland fell under Nazi control, as had already happened in Norway and Denmark.

The situation in France was particularly difficult and sensitive, because many Jewish German emigrants living there as refugees after 1933 were now threatened with imprisonment. What is more, French collaborators turned

Adolf Eichmann (above)
escaped to Argentina, and was
only arrested and sentenced to
death by Israel in 1960. Below:
Rudolf Höss, commandant of
Auschwitz, leaves the
Nuremberg courtroom in 1945.

against Jews in a shameful fashion, almost in anticipation of later German actions.

It is not known when the idea to confine Jews completely outside Europe, in a reserve in Madagascar, was abandoned. It had never been seriously pursued, nor was it easy to implement, since the island in the Indian ocean was outside German control. However, it is certain that at the time of the invasion of the Soviet Union — within the framework of the "vital space" in the east and the extreme brutality of methods that this implied — the prospect of the total physical elimination of Jews was already taken for granted.

The settling of scores with Judaism prophesied threateningly by the Nazis was in fact happening; it was, one could say, normal routine. The mass slaughter by the *Einsatzgruppen* of the SS and SD special units, who in a few weeks killed hundreds of thousands of Jews, went hand in hand with the triumphal German advance: a symbol of its success and a means of realizing the war objectives in the east.

It is through the Wannsee Protocol that we know the distribution of registered Jews in Europe, country by country. The protocol was produced during a conference at Wannsee on 20 January 1942 between two of Himmler's closest collaborators: Heydrich, head of the RSHA (the Central Office for Reich Security), and Adolf Eichmann, who were responsible for the Jewish department of the same RSHA. All these registered Jews — a total of eleven million individuals — were to be eliminated.

Yet the "final solution" was not decided at Wannsee; as far as the documentary evidence is concerned, the order to implement the "final solution" was given by Goering to Heydrich on 13 July 1941 — earlier than the Wannsee conference. On the basis of this order, concentration camps began to be systematically turned into extermination camps; in them would converge thousands of transports from all over occupied

Below: external view of the crematorium at Buchenwald concentration camp.
Ph. © Publiphoto

THE WANNSEE PROTOCOL

On 20 January 1942, at a conference at Grosser Wannsee, near Berlin, between the leaders of the security police and the departments involved in the operation under the supervision of Heydrich and Eichmann, plans for the final solution to the Jewish question were co-ordinated. The extermination was to concern the entire European Jewish population, a total of about eleven million people, divided as shown in the table. The Wannsee Protocol did not only include the countries already invaded by Germany (the A list), but also the Allied countries and Italy (the B list). ■

	Countries	No of Jews
A	Altreich (Germany)	131,800
	Eastern borderland (Austria)	43,700
	Eastern territories	420,000
	General Governorate (Poland)	2,284,000
	Bialystok	400,000
	Protectorate of Bohemia and Moravia	74,200
	Estonia (without Jews)	—
	Latvia	3,500
	Lithuania	34,000
	Belgium	43,000
	Denmark	5,600
	France — occupied territory	165,000
	— non-occupied territory	700,000
	Greece	69,600
	Holland	160,800
	Norway	1,300
B	Bulgaria	48,000
	Great Britain	330,000
	Finland	2,000
	Ireland	4,300
	Italy (including Sardinia)	58,000
	Albania	200
	Croatia	40,000
	Portugal	3,000
	Romania (including Bessarabia)	342,000
	Sweden	8,000
	Serbia	10,000
	Slovakia	88,000
	Spain	6,000
	Turkey (European area)	55,500
	Hungary	742,800
	Soviet Union	5,000,000
	Ukraine	2,994,684
	White Russia (excluding Bialystok)	446,484
	Total	over 11,000,000

Europe, from west to east.

In September 1941 the first mass killings with gas took place in Auschwitz: this system worked, and from then on the eliminations could proceed with industrial rhythm and technology. Rudolf Höss, the Auschwitz camp commandant, has left the most chilling account of the process.

The main extermination camps were situated in the occupied Polish territories: Chelmno, Belzec, Treblinka, Sobibor, Auschwitz and Majdanek. This was not by chance: a veritable trap for Jews, the big ghettos in Poland proved to be the antechambers of the extermination camps.

Two guards stand by containers filled with the gas which would be pumped into the "death rooms". In Auschwitz they used Zyklon B (hydrogen cyanide). Below: the arrival of a Jewish convoy in Auschwitz.
Ph. © Publiphoto

The deportations and transfers to extermination camps, which climaxed in the spring and summer of 1942, were implemented with astonishing synchronization and symmetry. From all over Europe, in an almost continuous stream, groups of deported people converged on the big death factories, places of unspeakable suffering

A dramatic picture showing the inhuman conditions in which prisoners were transported to concentration camps. Sometimes they would travel for days, squeezed like animals into goods wagons locked from the outside.
Below: a woman in a serious state of prostration in the concentration camp of Sachsenhausen, near Oranienburg.
Ph. © Publiphoto

which are remembered in eye-witness accounts of undoubted literary and human value, among them that of Primo Levi.

Upon arrival in the camps, prisoners were selected for extermination; those who survived the first selection were destined to expend their energies in forced labour for the Third Reich. Only a few survived illness, hunger, exhaustion and the humiliations of sadistic scientific experiments which went hand in hand with the premeditated genocide of the Jewish population.

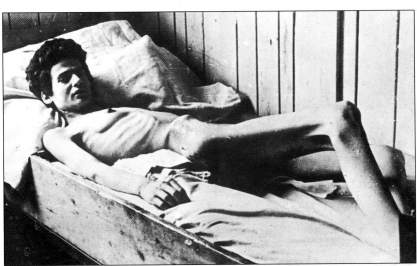

A street in the Warsaw ghetto. Opened in October 1939, the Warsaw Jewish ghetto had about 450,000 inhabitants. From 22 July 1942 the Nazis began to deport the ghetto's population to extermination camps: at a rate of about 6,000–9,000 per day, Jews from Warsaw were put on trains directed to Treblinka, where the majority died in the gas chambers. The final blow to the ghetto came on 19 April 1943: a column of 2,000 SS, with tanks and artillery, began the final evacuation. They were unexpectedly opposed by the Jewish Fighting Organization, led by Mordecai Anielewicz, who resisted the Nazis until 8 May.

In March 1942 a great wave of deportations from Slovakia began; in July came big raids on Paris and Amsterdam, and also the mass evacuation of the Warsaw ghetto, the greatest concentration of Jews in central Europe; in March 1943 Greece followed; on 16 October 1943 there was a raid on the Rome ghetto, now controlled by the Wehrmacht; between April and May 1944 it was the turn of the Hungarian Jews; after Hungary followed Italy.

These are only a few of the main stages marking the last phase of the "final solution", without counting "wild" slaughters and individual and mass executions carried out as SS and Wehrmacht formations combed the occupied territories. It was a tale of destruction punctuated by occasional episodes of heroic resistance, such as the uprising of the Warsaw ghetto (April–May 1943), stifled by the Germans in the bloodiest manner with the help of collaborating Ukranian and Latvian units. The anti-Semitic ferocity of these latter troops revealed the deep divisions in the civil and human fabric of Europe upon which the destructive fury of Nazism depended.

Among the many problems raised by the Jewish tragedy — for the conscience of all humanity, and not only for historians — is undoubtedly the question of why nobody intervened to stop Germany's destructive work. Although the knowledge of what was happening under German occupation was only approximate, it was sufficient to allow nobody the justification of ignorance. It is difficult to find an answer to this question, and it raises the perturbing doubt that the interests of power and strategic calculations could have prevented intervention to oppose the murderous project.

Finally, it is worth mentioning the statistical balance of genocide. In spite of the fragmented sources of information and the attempts made *in extremis* by the Nazis to hide, when and where possible, the traces of their crimes, the evidence gathered over decades of research give us an idea of the dimensions of the genocide, if not the full picture. The figure announced by the Nuremberg international tribunal, which estimated the number of murdered Jews at about six million, has stood the test of time and resisted all attempts at revision, even if the most recent and reliable research puts the number of victims at between a minimum of 5,300,000 and a maximum of just over six million.

Concentration camp prisoners celebrate their liberation by Allied troops.

Chapter 8

FROM **T**OTAL **W**AR TO **T**OTAL **D**EFEAT

WITH THE DECLARATION OF "TOTAL WAR" THE NAZI REGIME
PLAYED ITS LAST DESPERATE CARD BEFORE ITS FINAL SURRENDER.
ON 30 APRIL 1945 HITLER COMMITTED SUICIDE IN THE
REICHSTAG BUNKER, THUS ESCAPING SOVIET ARREST. THOSE
RESPONSIBLE FOR NAZI CRIMES WERE JUDGED BY THE ALLIED
FORCES AT THE NUREMBERG TRIBUNAL.

During the first months of the war, the regime intensified the use of its repressive apparatus on a general scale. It managed to secure an adequate level of foodstuffs and consumer goods for the population, thereby maintaining their compliance while simultaneously requiring a greater effort in mobilization and making the dictatorship's grip more inflexible and widespread. From 3 September 1939 a series of provisions implemented a strategy of maximizing the war effort and, at the same time, maintaining cohesion behind the regime: one of the first measures was to ban listening to foreign radio broadcasts on pain of serious punishment, as the enemy radio was considered to be an instrument deliberately transmitting lies aimed at dividing the German people.

The powers of the security police were also strengthened and extended, so that they could take action against anybody who appeared to be a threat to the system: "Every effort to break the unity and the fighting will of the German people must be stifled mercilessly. Whoever with his words puts the victory of the German people, or its

After the fall of Berlin on 2 May 1945, Admiral Dönitz, nominated by Hitler as his successor just before his suicide in the Reichstag bunker, signed the unconditional surrender to the Allied forces on 8 May; hostilities ceased on 9 May, after a massive bombardment which preceded the occupation of Prague by the Red Army.
Opposite: American soldiers march through a German city destroyed by bombing.

right to war, into doubt, must be immediately arrested."

The third step in the establishment of war discipline was a whole set of measures which were designed on the one hand to keep the productive system efficient, and on the other to maintain a

From the beginning of Nazism, the SS had represented the regime's élite avant-garde, capable of ensuring order and security for the Reich by any means. Above: an SS rally at the Nuremberg stadium.
Ph. © Publiphoto
Right: propaganda to raise funds for the armed forces.

good standard of living. The first measure was an order on the war economy proclaimed on 3 September.

The Discipline of Total War

A police regime, propaganda pressure and a punctilious social policy were thus the instruments used to maintain the greatest possible consensus around the war effort. During its victorious phase, the Third Reich applied this strategy with success. The immediate rationing of essential foods and the most necessary consumer goods was introduced to avoid shortages and discontent among the population — beyond that rendered unavoidable by the adoption of measures such as longer working hours and the like. Partial self-sufficiency ensured a good basic diet from the outset; later, with the acquisition of occupied territories, the German people would enjoy throughout the war a diet which was superior (often considerably superior) to that of the rest of the European population. For example, the importation into Germany of food reserves from Denmark (especially animal fat) represented a constant flow of produce which the Reich exploited in a practised manner until the end of hostilities.

Stock accumulated through the plundering of occupied territories was another safety valve created at the expense of other peoples. The control of prices was intended to compensate workers for a wage freeze, which on the surface avoided the need for more rigid measures such as wage reduction, but which in practice involved unpaid overtime and thus a net loss in earnings — another way to finance war expenditure.

Restrictions on consumer goods and the changes caused by the war regime did not manifest themselves immediately. On the other hand,

Soon after the outbreak of war, essential food rationing was introduced for the whole German population. In the picture, milk rations are distributed in a small town in Germany.
Ph. © Publiphoto

the call to arms for men involved an enormous mobilization of manpower and had a direct impact on German society. The widespread introduction of female labour for war production (in agriculture, but above all in industry) was a substantial change in the role previously assigned by Nazism to women — who had been seen up until then as the mere reproducers of the race and guardians of the family and tradition.

This change in direction, which had already begun on the eve of war, intensified as the conflict developed and dragged on. On 27 January 1943 the regime ordered that work was compulsory for all men aged between sixteen and sixty-five and women aged between seventeen and forty-five, as part of a policy of mobilizing all previously-unexploited resources promoted by *Gauleiter* Sauckel, appointed commissioner for manpower issues in March 1942. The level of female employment was very high by this time, approaching the peak it reached in 1944, when women working in the production system represented almost half the total labour force. Eventually the war effort even involved young people, who were mobilized for war duties on 2 December 1943, after Goebbels's declaration of "total war".

*T*he prolonged war necessitated the use of all the available workforce: in 1944 female workers accounted for almost half the total. Young boys of the Hitlerjugend, who underwent proper military training after their recruitment into the organization, were sent to the front by Hitler in the last desperate phase of the German retreat.
Above: women at work in an arms factory.
Right: Hitler Youth members receive training from a Luftwaffe pilot.
Ph. © Publiphoto

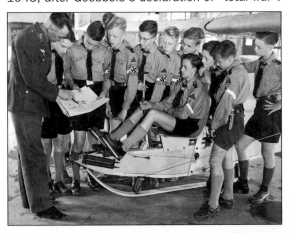

The survival of the home front was largely due to the firm social and political cohesion, in which ideology and the *Volksgemeinschaft* organization played a major part. The role of propaganda was also significant. Goebbels and his organization assaulted the German people with daily propaganda, establishing essential support. While Germany was winning the war, Goebbels encouraged ruthlessness against the enemy and exulted in the aerial war against Britain; when war events showed signs of a reversal, he railed against the enemies of Germany, blaming them for suffocating the country with the weapons of international Judaism and Bolshevism. When, in the spring of 1942, the aerial offensive against Germany intensified, reducing the main German cities to ruins, Goebbels took on the task of spurring the population of the affected areas on to a "satanic hatred", a "satanic obsession", a "fanatical determination" and a "satanic will to destroy" the enemy.

Doctor Josef Goebbels, Propaganda Minister of the Reich, was the last in the hierarchy to abandon the Führer in the days of defeat; entrenched in the Reichstag bunker, he, together with Hitler and his family, committed suicide on 1 May 1945.

On 30 January 1943, the tenth anniversary of Nazism's rise to power and the eve of the battle of Stalingrad, Goebbels launched the slogan of "total war" at the Berlin sports hall, complete with threats against the external enemy and even more against those who did not expend their last energies for the war effort. Forgetting his earlier appeal to their attacking capabilities, he now presented the conflict as a "war of national defence", increasing the threatening tension in his speech to the point of suggesting a — by then unattainable — "final total victory". The fact that at the height of the crisis in July 1944 caused by the attempt on the Führer's life on 20 July, Hitler appointed Goebbels commissioner for total war was not only a recognition of his services, but above all a sign of the importance of propaganda. Its energetic inducement to the people was a real support for the war effort.

The Russian campaign proved much more difficult than previous invasions; the severe weather conditions during the winter of 1941–42 made it impossible to advance until the following spring, thus giving the Russians the opportunity to organize a counteroffensive. During this campaign a large number of soldiers died from exposure: winter uniforms were not available, as Hitler had not predicted that the operation could last until winter.
Below: a German guard tries to take shelter from the cold.

Internal Disagreements and Dissension

Germany did not experience the armed resistance which characterized the behaviour of the peoples involved in the invasion and war everywhere in occupied Europe. This does not mean that there was no domestic opposition to Nazism between its rise to power and its defeat. The lightning speed of repression against real or potential enemies from the Nazis' first weeks in power, and the creation of a powerful, destructive and widespread system of control and repression, largely explain why internal opposition in Germany was not as significant as in other areas outside the country. They also explain why Germany did not free itself from the Nazi dictatorship by its own means. Strong support for the regime's policies of patriotism and conquest contributed to the isolation of the active opposition minorities. The opposition centred around a potential reconstruction of traditional parties, especially the two workers' parties, the Communists and the Social Democrats; around relevant personalities in the higher administration, who as representatives of conservative, liberal or Christian forces saw in Nazism an offence against the constitutional state; around representatives of the Wehrmacht, aware that Germany had engaged in a suicidal war and also of the damage done to human rights and international law by the way the war was conducted by the Nazis; and around Church representatives. But there is no space here to review in detail the individual opposition groups, nor to outline the profiles of some of its most significant representatives.

It has already been argued that the mobilization for war involved an intensity of repression in view of a possible

increase in open opposition or, more probably, discontent and widespread dissent against the war, which could have affected the unity of the people. Indeed, as the war dragged on after the first triumphs and its sacrifices impinged on the population, its consequences became visible at home, with the terror and destruction caused by the aerial blitz as well as gloomy rumours of reversals from the front. Their culmination was the German defeat at Stalingrad, which brought the anguish of war directly into German homes, along with the evidence of losses, a disbelief in the regime's promises, and finally doubts over the justness of the cause.

Infiltrating among the people, official representatives and informers of the Gestapo reported that the population (*Volksgenossen*, in the informers' bureaucratic jargon) no longer seemed to understand the strategic importance of Stalingrad and the necessity of sacrificing so many lives without a timely withdrawal. In particular, there appeared to be a "general conviction that Stalingrad marked a turning point in the war". In the reports from the

Above: a pincer movement by the Red Army cuts off Hitler's claws (from a Soviet poster circulated during the counteroffensive).
Left: "A toast to Hitler", a postcard dropped by the Russians over the German lines. In the first six months of the campaign the Wehrmacht lost 775,000 men dead, wounded or taken prisoner.

security service, the weakest tended to "see in the Stalingrad defeat the beginning of the end". In comparison with reports immediately after the invasion of the USSR, with their triumphant comments and acclamation of the Führer for having been able to prevent and unmask the Bolsheviks' aggressive intentions, public opinion had changed radically.

The population was no longer united, and the measures to mobilize labour were now greeted with scepticism; it was thought that unfairness in treatment had increased and that the division of sacrifices among the population were, as usual, at the expense of the vulnerable. In particular, women among the lower classes wondered if the wives of notables (the *Prominenten*) would also have to share the sufferings of an increasingly difficult daily life. The result was a German society which no longer corresponded to the stereotypes and the smooth and shining image of the "people's community". Some historians have compared the German state of mind at this stage to that of a survivor; in other words, if the regime could still count on some solidarity, it was dictated by the will to survive of a nation which had no choice but to accept the present passively.

Underground Movements and Organizations

Yet not everybody passively accepted the *status quo*. The Gestapo continued to arrest thousands and thousands of people every year — in 1941 alone, those arrested for Communist or Social Democratic activities totalled 11,410, quite apart from those arrested for other reasons; in 1942, 10,613 arrests were recorded for the same political reasons, again without counting the other "enemies" of the Reich.

The Jews were now deported on a daily basis; they were often marched through the cities in columns before being put into railway wagons, under the indifferent eyes of the population.

Deportees and forced labourers, both civilians and prisoners of war, were used to clear the ruins of the destroyed cities. Many Germans did not want to acknowledge the significance of these everyday sights, but others saw them as an offence against the human rights of other nationalities and above all an insult to the German nation, and they refused to accept the situation. Among those who first reacted were the young students gathered around the "White Rose" in Munich: Hans and Sophie Scholl, their friends Willi Graf and Alexan-

INTERNAL OPPOSITION TO THE REGIME

Internal opposition to National Socialism has often been underestimated, since Germany did not experience the spontaneous mass uprisings, and even less the armed struggle against the regime, which occurred in occupied Europe and Italy in the form of the Resistance. This does not mean that there was no political rebellion, circulation of illegal propaganda (often smuggled into the country by anti-Nazi émigrés), or passive resistance; all these existed, and would proliferate with the worsening of the situation on the domestic front during the war.

Tough Nazi repression from the first weeks after their rise to power, with the arrest and deportation of thousands of officers and representatives of the labour movement and other political parties — the regime's potential natural opponents — badly affected any future efforts to maintain an illegal network of Social Democrats and Communists. For this reason, among others, it was easiest for opposi-

tion to grow in the heart of the system itself: it often emanated from rebellious elements within the administration or the diplomatic corps, and from representatives of the armed forces working within the power structure of the regime. The discontent caused by the war spread among the younger generation and was the cause of some truly heroic opposition movements, such as the students

Colonel Klaus von Stauffenberg, an officer on the general staff, was responsible for the attempt on Hitler's life on 20 July 1944.

gathered around the Munich Weisse Rose (White Rose) group, who were also moved by a strong religious spirit; they were executed between February and April 1943.

The path followed by the opposition groups, and not only the conservatives, was more complex. A plot by representatives of the Wehrmacht led to the attempt on Hitler's life on 20 July 1944; its failure caused an unprecedented outburst of repression, eliminating a substantial group of the traditional élites who had once been in line with the regime, but who now kept their distance in view of the war's disastrous outcome and the horror of the crimes committed by the Reich throughout Europe.

Within this framework there was also opposition from religious people who, distancing themselves from the passive or neutral attitude of the institutional Churches, felt sympathy for the victims of the Nazis' political and racial persecution. ■

When it became clear that the German army was collapsing, the number of soldiers surrendering or deserting rose, despite Hitler's order to kill anybody who left their unit for any reason.
Above: German soldiers in civilian clothes slaughtered by the SS while they were trying to escape.
Ph. © Publiphoto
Below: a poster from Berlin in the 1930s — a blacklist of women who continued to shop in Jewish stores.

der Schmorell, and a professor of philosophy at Munich University, Kurt Huber.

Motivated by deep religious feelings linked to Catholicism, and by a determination to redeem the name of the German nation, the students in the White Rose circle began an active campaign of information and protest in spring 1942. Their leaflets highlighted the need for profound domestic reform to save Germany. Today it is known that the group around the Scholls was more widespread than was initially thought; they were testimony to the existence of a potential opposition which would grow with the worsening of the war situation.

The group went beyond the simple distribution of leaflets and appealing for passive opposition; at the peak of the crisis, between the end of 1942 and the beginning of 1943 and thus under the pressure of the Stalingrad tragedy, they did not hesitate to launch an open appeal to sabotage the war effort. This gesture clearly went far beyond mere internal criticism or rumour-mongering: it demonstrated a concrete, practical rebellion and also a desire for freedom from the control exercised by the *Hitlerjugend* upon the youngest in society.

In mid-February 1943 Hans and Sophie Scholl were arrested, tried, sentenced to death, and executed on 18 February. Though they were humiliated and summarily beheaded, the Scholls and their White Rose group showed that opposition was spreading to sectors which, for political or cultural reasons, or even only on grounds of age, had not previously been affected. A few months before the Gestapo had eliminated the Red Orchestra (*Rote Kapelle*) underground organization, one of the most resourceful and politicized among the illegal groups, linked to the traditional Communist opposition and the labour movement. The setbacks in the war were now combined with other new areas of growing discontent. This, however, was not sufficient to create a popular movement; it increased insecurity within the regime, but did not create an alternative. This was the backdrop against which the plot to assassinate Hitler was carried out and bloodily stifled on 20 July 1944.

Above: the meeting room in the Rastenburg after the explosion of von Stauffenburg's bomb, designed to kill the Führer. Below: American troops landing in Normandy.

Defeat

The creation of a Second Front on the part of the anti-Nazi coalition, with the landings in Normandy on 6 June 1944, opened the final stage of the war against Germany, and also precipitated the final phase within the regime. The pincer movements towards the heart of the Reich from both west and east, with the Red Army increasingly pushing the Wehrmacht westwards, meant that Germany now had to defend herself on her own territory. What is more, after the loss of the occupied territories she could now count only on her own forces and reserves.

As the two opposing sides showed no signs of conciliation — the Allies wanted nothing less than Germany's unconditional surrender, as had happened with Italy, and Germany was not prepared to get rid of the Nazi regime — it seemed that only Germany's total defeat could bring about the end of the war. But was it

*A*bove: Major Helmut Stieff was one of those responsible for the bomb which destroyed Hitler's headquarters. The reprisals against the authors of the plot were particularly brutal: Stieff was tortured by the SS and then hung with a piano wire.
Below left: Hitler, Goering and Mussolini after the assassination attempt; Hitler did not want to cancel the Duce's visit, which had been arranged for the same day. He even showed him the Rastenburg ruins and reconstructed the scenes preceding the explosion.
Below right: The Führer's angry expression after receiving news of the Stalingrad defeat.
Ph. © Publiphoto

still possible, in the summer of 1944, to stop the war and the ensuing human losses, given the certainty of the defeat of the Third Reich?

With this in view and in the hope of saving whatever was possible, on 20 July 1944 General von Stauffenberg planted a bomb at Hitler's headquarters, the *Wolfschanze* ("wolf's lair"). Killing the Führer would free the Wehrmacht from their oath of loyalty, thus allowing the handing over of powers to the opposition and paving the way for negotiations to stop the war. However, complications emerged, as there were disagreements amongst the conspirators about whether to concede unconditional surrender on all fronts, or to negotiate peace with the West and then use all their remaining military might in the East against the Bolsheviks.

The failure of the plot, both for technical reasons and through bad luck, made this last attempt a vain one; instead, it made the Nazi leadership realize that opposition in many shapes and forms was widespread, confirming its belief that military action was the only way to survive. The regime's reaction was brutal repression, involving some thousands of people, and especially revenge against the Wehrmacht. That is why, once again, the appeal to rally around the Führer led to a further concentration of power in the hands of Hitler's most trusted collaborators. The role

assigned to Goebbels in the conduct of total war has already been discussed; on another level, the appointment of Himmler (already chief of the SS and the police, and commissioner for the consolidation of the German race) as Reich Minister of the Interior allowed the unification of the most important executive functions for internal security in the hands of the person who had continually represented the quintessence of the regime's terrorist apparatus.

The regime's last success was marked by the use of missiles, mainly built by the deported labour force and launched against England. Their last crimes against the German people were committed with the conscription to the front of sixteen-year-old boys and old men, all gathered hastily around the so-called *Volkssturm,* in an extreme expression of national fanaticism. The events which followed illustrate the history of a regime which imploded, precipitating the ruin of the whole of Germany.

The resistance to the bitter end ordered by Hitler went beyond any reasonable expectation, and included a determination to reduce Germany to scorched earth, as had happened in the occupied territories; Himmler's order to evacuate concentration camps to the east caused the deaths of hundreds of thousands more deported prisoners during exhausting marches. All this highlights the decline of the Third Reich into a smouldering mass, like a symbol of the punishment of a regime built on the flames of the Reichstag.

Germany surrendered unconditionally on 8 May 1945, following the suicides of Hitler and Goebbels in the Chancellery bunker and the arrival of Soviet troops in Berlin. The surrender came after an extreme and ambiguous attempt by Admiral Dönitz to

The advancing Allied troops removed Hitler's image from the occupied territories. In the picture, a huge poster with Hitler's portrait is taken away on a truck.
Ph. © Publiphoto

ensure the survival of a German government after the downfall of a regime of which he had constituted one of the military pillars. The surrender put an end to the war and raised the problems of the dismantlement of the Nazi regime and of Germany's future. Germany's occupation by the Four Powers was the first step marking the disappearance of a German central authority after the defeat. Occupation also involved the division of Germany which, in the climate of the Cold War, led to the end of national unity. This was a direct consequence not only of defeat, but of the German responsibility for the outbreak of war and the sack of Europe.

The theme of responsibility for the war atrocities was the only decision which met with the unanimous agreement of all the victorious powers. The Nuremberg trials, which opened towards the end of 1945, were to judge those mainly responsible for the Nazi regime, who were charged with war crimes against humanity. The verdicts implied a total condemnation of the Nazi regime and marked the beginning of a historic legal settlement which, because of the size of the territory involved, the devastation caused and the huge numbers of victims, is to this day far from being concluded.

Germany's most important cities were destroyed by the Allied aerial bombardment.
Above: RAF bombers depicted in an British poster.
Right: the Chancellery in Berlin in May 1945, after the end of the fighting.

The Allies' intention to punish Nazi crimes was made clear from January 1941 onwards. In October 1942, with the joint participation of Great Britain, the United States and the Soviet Union, an inter-Allied commission on war crimes was created in London, followed by the Moscow Act of 30 October 1943 which laid the foundations for the Nuremberg international tribunal. The trials opened on 19 November 1945, and were based on three fundamental charges: crimes against peace (preparation for wars of invasion); war crimes (violation of war conventions and practices); and crimes against humanity (deportations, genocide, forced labour, reprisals, and so on). Apart from Hitler and other senior Nazis (Goebbels, Himmler and Ley) who had escaped Allied retribution by committing suicide, the highest representatives of the political and economic establishment and the highest military ranks of the Third Reich were put on trial.

Among Hitler's closest collaborators only one, Martin Bormann, was sentenced by default. On 10 October 1946 the verdicts of the international court were declared.

● Death sentence: Goering, von Ribbentrop, Rosenberg, Streicher, Kaltenbrunner, Frank, Sauckel, Seyss-Inquart, Frick, Keitel, Jodl, Bormann.

Above: a poster celebrates the Allied victory against Nazism. Below: a scene from the Nuremberg trials, and preparations for executing the death sentences.

● Life imprisonment: Raeder, Funk, Hess, Speer.
● Twenty years' imprisonment: von Schirach.
● Fifteen years' imprisonment: von Neurath.
● Ten years' imprisonment: Dönitz.
Schacht, von Papen and Fritsche were acquitted.
On 15 October 1946, in Nuremberg prison, the death sentences were executed (Goering had committed suicide after his sentence was announced). Many other sentences were pronounced by the military tribunals of Germany's occupying powers, in particular by American courts. However, after the beginning of the 1950s the Cold War prevented the operation of the Allied tribunals and substantial amnesties were granted for sentences already pronounced. Only at the end of 1958 did the German justice system begin to work systematically against the main Nazi crimes and criminals. ■

Bibliography

■ C. Bloch, *The Third Reich and the World, (Le III Reich et le monde)* Paris 1986

■ M. Broszat, *The Hitler State: The Foundation and Development of the Internal Structure of the Third Reich*, London 1982

■ A. Bullock, *Hitler, A Study in Tyranny*, London 1952

■ E. Collotti, *Nazi Germany, (La Germania nazista)* Turin 1962

■ E. Collotti, *Nazism and German Society 1933–1945, (Nazismo e societa tedesca 1933–1945)* Turin 1982

■ M. Gilbert, *The Holocaust, the Jewish Tragedy*, London 1986

■ M. Gilbert, *Auschwitz and the Allies*, London 1986

■ D. J. Goldhagen, *Hitler's Willing Executioners: Ordinary Germans and the Holocaust*, New York 1997

■ R. Griffin, *Fascism*, (Oxford readers) Oxford 1995

■ A. Hitler, *Mein Kampf*, trans. R. Manhein, New York 1950

■ I. Kershaw, *The "Hitler Myth". Image and reality in the Third Reich*, London 1987

■ L. Klinkhammer, *The German Occupation in Italy, 1943–1945*, Turin 1993

■ R. Lamb, *War in Italy 1943–1945: A Brutal Story*, New York 1996

■ P. Levi, *If Not Now When?*, London 1995

■ P. Levi, *Survival in Auschwitz: The Nazi Assault on Humanity*, London 1995

■ J. Lukacs, *The Hitler of History*, New York 1997

■ A. Milward, *The German Economy at War*, London 1965

■ L. Poliakov, J. Sabille, *Jews Under the Italian Occupation*, New York 1983

■ J. M. Palmier, *Weimar in Exile, (Weimar en exil)* Paris 1988

■ L. Richard, *Nazism and Culture, (Le nazisme et la culture)* Paris 1978

■ W. L. Shirer, *The Rise and Fall of the Third Reich*, London 1962

■ W. Sofsky, *The Order of Terror: The Concentration Camp*, Princeton 1996

■ A. Speer, *Inside the Third Reich*, London 1970

■ F. Taylor (Ed.), *The Goebbels Diaries 1939–1941*, London 1982

■ J. Toland, *Adolf Hitler*, New York 1992

■ H. R. Trevor-Roper, *The Last Days of Hitler*, London 1947

■ A. & J. Tusa, *The Nuremberg Trial*, London 1983

Chronology

1918 **9 November** The Kaiser's abdication. The Weimar Republic is born.
1919 **5 January** Anton Drexler founds the *Deutsche Arbeiterpartei*.
1920 **24 February** Drexler's party is renamed the NSDAP and announces a twenty-five point programme.
1921 **10 July** Hitler becomes leader of the NSDAP.
1923 **8–9 November** Failure of Hitler's putsch in Munich.
1924 **1 April** Sentenced to five years' imprisonment, Hitler is sent to the Landsberg fortress.
20 December Hitler is released.
1925 **27 February** The National Socialist Party, which had been banished after the 1923 putsch, is reorganized.
1928 **6 May** The National Socialist Party gains 2.6 per cent of the vote in the Reichstag elections.
1930 **23 January** The NSDAP controls a *Länd* government, in Thuringia, for the first time.
14 September In the Reichstag elections the NSDAP gains 18.3 per cent of the vote.
1931 **11 October** Harzburg Front of "national opposition" with the participation of the NSDAP.
1932 **13 March–10 April** In two ballots for the presidential elections, the NSDAP gains 30.1 and 36.8 per cent of the vote respectively (Hindenburg wins 49.6 and 53 per cent).
31 July In the Reichstag elections the NSDAP becomes the major party, winning 37.4 per cent of the vote.
6 November New Reichstag elections: the NSDAP falls back slightly with 33.1 per cent of the vote.
1933 **30 January** After the big industrial and financial groups withdraw their support for the Schleicher cabinet, President Hindenburg appoints Adolf Hitler as Chancellor.
28 February After the burning of the Reichstag the first repressive laws are issued against the enemies of National Socialism.
5 March Elections of terror: the NSDAP gets 43.9 per cent of the vote; its German nationalist allies get eight per cent.
23 March A Reichstag without opposition gives full powers to Hitler.
31 March First law against *Länder* autonomy.
1 April Jewish activities are boycotted.
7 April A law to purge bureaucracy discriminates against Jews.
22 June–5 July Destruction and self-destruction of all parties of the Weimar system.
14 July The NSDAP is proclaimed as the only legal party; a law for the protection of the race from hereditary diseases is issued.
20 July Concordat with the Holy See.
14 October Germany leaves the Society of Nations.
1934 **27 February** Law on the organization of "national labour".

30 June Settlement of accounts with the SA and murder of Röhm.

2 August After the death of Hindenburg, Hitler becomes President of the Reich.

1935 **13 January** Nazi triumph in the Saar plebiscite.

16 March Reintroduction of compulsory conscription.

15 September Nuremberg laws against the Jews.

1936 **7 March** The Reich reoccupies the Rhineland, which had been demilitarized by the Versailles Treaty.

28 July First intervention of German aircraft in the Spanish Civil War.

9 September The Four-Year Plan for the war economy is decided.

23 October The Rome—Berlin Axis is signed.

25 November Signing of the anti-Comintern pact with Japan.

1 December The *Hitlerjugend* becomes the state youth organization.

1937 **5 November** Conference between Hitler and military leaders: instructions are given for the invasion of Austria and Czechoslovakia.

1938 **4 February** Replacement of military leaders and the Foreign Minister in preparation for war.

12 March Austrian *Anschluss.*

30 September The Munich Pact returns the Sudetenland to Germany.

9 November "Night of Broken Glass" and pogroms against Jews.

1939 **15 March** Czechoslovakia invaded.

22 May Pact of Steel with Italy.

23 August Non-aggression pact with the USSR.

1 September Invasion of Poland and beginning of the Second World War.

1940 **14 June** The Wehrmacht enters Paris.

1941 **22 June** The invasion of the Soviet Union begins.

1942 **20 January** The Wannsee conference co-ordinates directives for the "final solution" to the Jewish question.

1943 **31 January** The Sixth German Army is defeated at Stalingrad.

18 February Goebbels declares "total war".

25 August Himmler is appointed Interior Minister of the Reich.

9 September After Italy's defeat the Wehrmacht occupies the territory of her erstwhile ally.

1944 **6 June** Anglo-American landing in Normandy.

20 July Attempt on Hitler's life in his headquarters.

1945 **4–11 February** The Yalta conference between Roosevelt, Churchill and Stalin decides that the Four Powers would occupy defeated Germany.

30 April Hitler commits suicide in the Chancellery bunker; Berlin invaded by the Red Army.

8 May Unconditional surrender of German armed forces.

17 July–2 August The Potsdam conference establishes the criteria for the Four Powers' occupation of Germany.

19 November Beginning of trials in front of the international military tribunal in Nuremberg.

Index of names

The Traveller's History Series

Printed in 1998 at Giunti Industrie Grafiche Stabilimento di Prato